SKILLED MIGRATION
CANADIAN EXPERIENCE

MYTHS AND REALITIES
THE GOOD THE BAD THE UGLY

ALABA OJAPINWA

Copyright (c) 2016
First Oasis Global Resources Ltd
Canada.
Tel: +1 587-437-1880

Nigeria.
Tel: +2348165848952
Email: wamiri@rocketmail.com
Website: firstoasisglobal.com

ISBN: 978-0-9952837-0-1

Interior Designed: Swapan Banik
Cover Design: Isaac Winston

Available at:
Major bookstores and Online at:
Amazon.com, Amazon.ca amazon.ng
Jumia.com
Rovingheights Nigeria
Alibaba.com
Konga
Dipdiscount

Email for quantity order requests can also be sent to:
wamiri@rocketmail.com

To all of the migrants who are striving to make life better for themselves and future generations.

CONTENTS

Acknowledgements	ix
Preface	xi
Why Write a Book on Skilled Migration?	xi
About The Author	xv
Setting Out	1
Migration	4
The Economic Migrant	7
Economic Migration Myths and Realities	8
Migration Myths and Realities	11
Myth 1	13
Economic Migrants Leave Their Country for Better Financial Status.	13
Myth 2	16
Migrants Steal Jobs of Natives	16
Myth 3	21
Economic Migrants Lower Wages	21
Myth 4	23
Migrants Scout for Benefits and are an Economic Burden to Host Country.	23
Myth 5	26
Migrating to the Western World Makes Life and Financial Freedom Much Easier.	26
Myth 6	31
Migrants are a Security Risk to the Host Country	31

v

Migration The Good — 35
- Human Capacity Development — 37
- Better Infrastructure and Technology — 41
- Security — 53
- Remittances — 54
- Competiveness — 55
- Cultural Diversity, Multiculturalism and Inclusiveness. — 57
- Skill and Technology Transfer — 60
- Better Political Culture, Leadership, Follower Ship and Government. — 60
- Government Social and Community Support for the Financially, Physically, and Mentally Handicapped. — 65

Migration the Bad — 67
- Non-Integration — 69
- Poor Skilled Job Prospects — 73
- My Job Search Experience — 87
- Foreign Credentials and Experience not Generally Recognized. — 98
- Difficulty in Profitably Running Small Family Businesses — 122
- Huge Household Debts/Non-Remittance — 128
- Loss of Family, Social Ties, and Cultural Identity. — 133

Migration the Ugly — 135
- Anti-Migrant Sentiments — 137
- Family Separation and Breakdown — 146
- Loss of Cultural Identity, Family, and Cultural Values — 146
- Narrowing of the Middle Class due to Capitalism — 155
- Individualistic Culture and Loneliness — 157
- High Degree of Freedom, Personal Choice and Right Promoting Instability. — 158

The Right Thing To Do — a Personal Reflection — 167
- The Prospective Migrant — 167
  1. Do not migrate irregularly (without proper documentation) — 167
  2. Be sure that you possess the skills needed in the target country. — 168
  3. Do Not Resign Your Job or Sell Your Business and Properties Until You are Sure You Would Fit into Economic Activities in Your New Country. — 169
  4. Do Not Have Social Welfare of Host Country in Mind While Moving There. — 170
  5. Make an Effort to Avoid Family Separations — 171
  6. Design an Exit Strategy — 171

To Source Country and People	173
Practical Commitment to the Social Welfare of Citizens	178
Followership and Dependents	180
What Host Countries Should Do	181
Ascertain the Need Before Bringing in Skilled Migrants	183
Reducing Global Inequities and Promoting World Peace	**186**
Doing It Right	**191**
How It Works	192
Conclusion	**194**
Index	**197**

ACKNOWLEDGEMENTS

I sincerely appreciate the many people who have called, written and e-mailed me on several occasions asking about skilled migration to Canada.

I spent thousands of hours in phone calls, emails and other media responding to these requests.

This motivated me to incorporate my views, opinions, and experiences into a book. They inspired me in this effort to satisfy their curiosity. My goal was to present my experience in a clear manner for all prospective skilled migrants. As they plan for their future and those of their loved ones, making decisions and taking actions on this potentially impactful and life changing endeavor of skilled migration, it is my hope this piece will be helpful.

I drew inspiration and support from many other resources to bring this effort to fruition. Thank God for Canada, arguably the best country in the world and great Nigeria for providing the template for this work.

I would like to thank my life partner Eniola, for her support, love encouragement, prayers and other contributions. To my children Bolu, Omoluabi and Ire, thank you for letting me deny you some attention while I was working on this. I love you guys.

To my brother Taiwo, my brothers from other mothers, Henry Oloja, Dr. Abdullah Habeebu, Dayo Lomuwagun, and to Anthony Adesina,

David Mbong and Roger Agard, thank you all for your great help and suggestions.

Stephen Weiner, thank you for your help in making this work more reader friendly.

Winston Isaac for the cover page, and Swapan Banik for putting all together into a beautiful whole, my appreciation.

My ultimate gratitude goes to Almighty God who has preserved us thus far.

Alaba Ojapinwa

July 2016.

PREFACE

Why Write a Book on Skilled Migration?

Canada is a fantastic country and arguably the best place on planet earth where anybody would want to live, raise a family or die. I came to this conclusion after a personal, very thorough and unbiased assessment of a number of factors. By the same token, Canada has many attractions for a skilled migrant. This is the position of many people around the world. In the words of my brother when this topic came up between us, "it is not easy to build such a nation with so much enduring, enviable, functional institutions and humanistic values. However, it is not fun for many people who are rushing to Canada". I agree fully with him.

This is an especially logical conclusion for some of us who have had the unenviable "privilege" of seeing life in other climes. The benefit of such a dual and almost opposite experience is a blessing since it allows us to have a global and balanced view of issues. It enables us to appreciate both sides better.

But is Canada Eldorado for a skilled migrant? Is success and fulfilment taken for granted in Canada? What are those things that a skilled migrant should know and keep in mind as he undertakes this great endeavor? What are the challenges and opportunities for the skilled migrant? What attitudes, thoughts and actions should the host residents, citizens, and government cultivate for best outcomes? What should be the roles, attitudes and thought processes of family, friends, associates and government in the country of origin of the skilled migrants so that this experience and undertaking brings about the best outcome for all stakeholders?

Over the past five years, the subject of skilled migration has been a very significant aspect of my life. The migration experience has been life transforming. The process has had a profound impact on my life and that of my family. The impact has been a mixed bag. Future events will determine if this experience has been worthwhile.

A considerable amount of physical, material, financial and psychological effort has gone into the process of getting to this stage. We have enjoyed goodwill, and encouragement from our new country, family, friends, and others. As a result, I have a passable understanding and enlightenment on this subject.

Based on my own experience and that of others, I have learned some valuable information to share with prospective migrants or others in the form of a book.

It is futile for any society to tell people not to migrate. This is because migration is part of human nature. It would even be more futile to discourage migration to Canada. If anybody needs to move out of his country, Canada comes up as preferred for obvious reasons. It has an enviable pedigree for it to earn that reputation. It is more expedient to provide people with the tools and resources to stimulate conversations that can engender informed decisions, so that migration can be as worthwhile an experience as possible.

I am inundated daily by questions from individuals who are interested in this topic. This is my way of solving a personal problem which is having to answer the same questions daily. It has, therefore, become imperative for me to tell prospective skilled migrants how I see it. This book is a hard reference that will be available to everyone so that they can form their own ideas.

Preface

This is not an attempt to tell people what to do. It is an effort to shine more light on this issue so that people can see other perspectives. To some, it is a new conversation started, while to some others, it is just the same or another view of what they are already familiar with.

This book represents my current personal opinion. This opinion is not evergreen. It is a continuously evolving subject. The dynamics of migration change frequently as do the situations, values, and aspirations of would-be migrants. The issue of migration is fluid, heterogeneous and convoluted. Individual experiences, situations and circumstances differ. Therefore, there is the need for a great deal of individualization of the processing of the information. This book is not an attempt to tell my readers what they have not read, heard or thought of before but to further help bring these things to our consciousness. I am not claiming to be an expert, and my opinions can change with time, situations, and prevailing policies.

However, I feel qualified to write about this issue because I have experienced it firsthand. As they say, "who feels it, knows it". The experience of a skilled migrant is my personal story.

This is an attempt to challenge the myths surrounding economic migration rather than perpetuating them. I believe it is crucial to examine all of the aspects of migration so that prospective migrants see a wider and more detailed picture.

By presenting this information, this book will make several aspects of economic migration clearer to readers so they can make better informed and more rational choices.

I am aware of the diminishing popularity of the print media due to the constant draw and appeal of the new media—Google, Facebook, Twitter, and other digital interfaces as sources of information for people. I sometimes think maybe this should have been presented electronically for a larger audience. I am considering doing that sometimes in the future.

Nevertheless, it is my hope this print version will still find a good readership.

Come along with me as we turn the pages to reflect together on these issues.

God bless.

ABOUT THE AUTHOR

Alaba Ojapinwa is a skilled Nigerian-Canadian migrant.

He is a pharmacist who delves into writing whenever he gets a strong conviction to put his opinions and views down to serve as conversation point to interested stakeholders.

Providing conversation starters from his own exposure, experience and knowledge so people have a smooth experience as possible is his passion.

His first book *"The Heights That Great Men Reach"* was inspired to engender this kind of conversation for the future generation.

His third effort is in the works.

SETTING OUT

Life is a decision-making endeavor. From a point in life, it's all about decision making and dealing with the consequences of our decisions, good or bad. There are consequences to family, friends, the environment, humanity and us.

The baby has to make a decision to suckle mother's breast or not. The young man or woman at a certain point has to make a decision about career, marriage and relationships and whether or not to have children. Career change, when to retire etc. are decisions that we have to make at different points in our lives. There are also spirituality decisions. Some people would like to and do make decisions about how and when to die.

The decision to migrate, by leaving one's place of birth and primary abode and relocating to a new country is definitely a huge, significant and potentially life changing endeavor.

I just returned from buying food at the African market. My daughter who was nine years old saw me buy yams.

She asked: "What is this?"

Surprised, I replied: "Yams. Don't you know?"

That was unnecessary. If she knew, would she have asked?

"No," she replied.

"What do you mean?" I wondered aloud.

"Is this the yam we eat?" She asked.

'Yes," I replied.

Apparently, she did not know about the yam tuber. She has been eating yams, but I guess she had not been frequenting the kitchen for safety reasons. She had no idea what yams looked like whole before they were cooked.

"Oh, I didn't know this is how it looks."

"It looks like big potato," she enthused.

This got me thinking. Really? When I was eight, even though we were not professional farmers in our family, we always had farms for subsistence and grew a number of crops. My father could pass for a professional farmer even though he was a school principal when I was growing up and my mother would want to cultivate any available piece of land even when she later took on teaching as a profession after her children were all grown. At my daughter's age, I had a small farm where I had already planted and harvested yams. And I remember vividly they were yellow yams. She had been eating yams, but i guess.

As I write this, a thought is racing through my mind. This is to the effect I have actually spent 5 years outside my home country Nigeria and in Canada.

"5 years!!! You call that only?" A voice silently mused inside me.

"Yes, and no," another voice replied silently.

Yes, after 5 years, I should have seen and known enough to write on this, I said to myself.

But what is enough? This can be subjective. I run the risk of somebody having the opinion that five years is too short a time for one to have an informed opinion about this type of issue.

Setting Out

I consider myself to be an open minded and patient person who would always want to take in as much information and data as possible about an issue before forming an opinion about it. I have been doing that on this issue for a while now.

However, by waiting longer, I also run the risk of over-processing facts and delaying the release of a very strong urge to put this in print. There is also a risk of not having time to do this in the future since I see myself getting busier every day.

This is because the scarcest commodity, especially in this part of the world, is time. Everything, including wages, are time related. Time is the greatest limiting factor on getting things done anywhere in the world. The prospect of not being able to do this due to lack of time in the future is unimaginable to me.

I also have a strong feeling that my brain may "explode" if I don't let out the content of this book. It has been occupying a portion of my brain and yearning to get out.

I must confess that a part of me is ashamed of just coming up with this now. Over the past 5 years, I have logged over five thousand hours on the internet and phone calling, receiving calls, sending and receiving text messages and e-mails answering questions about this subject. A book on this topic would, therefore, have been a good and more efficient reference material. It would have represented my view on this more effectively and efficiently and would have made life easier for all of us. This is my own printed opinion on this today, and my way of answering a question confronting many people of my generation.

I must point out that my views expressed in this book are not permanent or unchangeable. Opinions and facts on these issues change with time depending on the prevailing policies and circumstances. This situation is no different.

It is my sincere hope, therefore, that the reader of this piece will be able to understand me in this context. This will allow them to form a rational opinion combined with expected consultation from other sources while considering each individual's specific circumstances.

Migration

Migration is the movement of people from their country of birth or where they have lived before to another country with the intention of settling and living there for a considerable length of time or permanently.

By settling in the new country, some become permanent residents while others will adopt or acquire the citizenship of their new country. As a result, this becomes the home country for their future generations.[1]

Why do people migrate?

These are some of the reasons why people migrate:

- Economic reasons
- Security reasons

Escape from:

- Political persecution
- Religious persecution
- War, conflicts, and disasters
- Gender preference persecution and many other forms of persecution

For improved personal and family capacity building and development.

For family cohesion and re-unification and many other reasons depending on the circumstances and values of the prospective immigrants.

---

[1] Wikipedia, the free encyclopedia; Human Migration (accessed December 10, 2015) https://en.wikipedia.org/wiki/wiki/HumanMigration.

According to Ban Ki-Moon, United Nations Secretary General "migration is an expression of the human aspiration for dignity, safety, and a better future. It is part of the social fabric, part of our very make-up as a human family."[2]

"And among man's personal rights we must include his right to enter a country in which he hopes to be able to provide more fittingly for himself and his dependents. It is therefore the duty of state officials to accept such immigrants and- so far as the good of their own community rightly understood, permits,-to further the aims of those who may wish to become members of a new society."[3]

The push-pull sociological model of migration is popular and favoured by many. This reckons migrants as one of the major factors of demographic development. Push factors are the negatives forcing people to migrate out of their home countries while pull factors are positives attracting migrants to their new country.

This model clearly distinguishes between migration for work and other economic reasons, which is voluntary, and migration for flight (refugee, protection etc.), which is involuntary.

When the pull factors aggregate, become attractive enough, and the opportunity and means becomes available, the tendency is for the subject to migrate.

It is an obvious fact that the world is trying to cope with the problem of overpopulation. Over 7 billion people inhabit the earth. This is very

---

[2] News and Media United Nations Radio. Remarks by Ban Ki-Moon, United Nations Secretary General to A High Level Dialogue on International Migration and Development, October 3, 2013. (accessed March 5, 2016) unmultimedia.org.

[3] Libreria Editrice Vaticana. Pacem In Terris; Encyclical of Pope John XXIII On Establishing Universal Peace In Truth, Justice, Charity and Liberty, n 106, April 11, 1963 w2vatican.va/content/John-XXIII/encyclicals/documents/hf-j-xxiii_enc_11041963=pacem.html (accessed March 20, 2016)

important when we think of resource distribution, poverty reduction, climate change, inequalities etc.

Ironically, the resource poor areas or less developed areas of the world tend to have a disproportionately high population.

Migration in any form and especially when well-coordinated might be a way of solving one of the modern world's greatest problems. This means the legitimate migration of people from densely populated but less developed areas of the world to areas that are sparsely populated but more developed. This can go a long way to help humanity.

A critical historical look at the various reasons that people migrate would reveal that it has primarily been in search for better economic prospects for the individual(s) and their future generations. In the face of increasing waves of terrorism, conflict and natural disasters, other forms of migration are assuming greater proportions. The high number of asylum seekers due to various reasons in different parts of the word readily comes to mind.

Humans are naturally wired to seek better deals for themselves. From creation through evolution, we have the natural tendency and propensity to seek better conditions and opportunities for ourselves.

Drawing from Abraham Maslow's theory of hierarchy of needs from basic needs such as physiological needs and safety to that of sense of love/belonging, self-esteem and self-actualization, we have always struggled and aspired to get a better deal for ourselves and our loved ones.

Towards this end, the grass has always seemed greener on the other side of the field. Humans have a tendency to take a peep through the fence or curtain that separates our field from the other pasture, to look outside our immediate environment in the hope of catching a glimpse of a ray of hope for better opportunities.

If we suspect that there is a better deal elsewhere and there is opportunity to move, the tendency is to be pre-occupied with the thought of moving, and eventually gravitate to taking actions to actualize this movement. This is an innate tendency of humans that is acquired from evolution, which the appropriate professional anthropologists, psycho-sociologists or others would be in a better position to explain.

The Economic Migrant

This can also be referred to as the work migrant. It describes someone who has migrated for reasons of securing a better job and improved financial status with the ultimate aim of a better standard of living.

Migrants are ordinary people who want a better life for themselves, their families and humanity. They are trying to make the world better by improving their individual and family lives.

Of all the various forms of migration, this is the most conscious and voluntary. This means that the actor has full control of the decision making process bringing him to the conclusion to move. He is also assumed to have a full control of the activities necessary to carry out the movement. It is his call and judgment. He has the inalienable right and opportunity to review this at any time during and after the process. He can make appropriate modifications, adjustments or reversals of his decision based on new knowledge and understanding that he may acquire along the way. These modifications might be informed by further consultations, revelations or changes in personal circumstances.

If the decision turns out to be worthwhile, he reserves the right to enjoy the results and the sense of accomplishment, satisfaction and fulfillment that comes with it.

Similar to all entrepreneurial endeavors, if it does not have a measurable positive impact on his life or if it has a negative impact on his economic, work and social status and standard of living, then he will have only himself to blame. This situation could turn out to be a real tragedy for the migrant. It is possible that he and loved ones would live to have a sense of regret.

The economic migrant must, therefore, be well schooled and enlightened about his choice and the likely implications, so he can make a well-informed decision on this significant life changing undertaking.

Economic Migration Myths and Realities

The idea of migrating to the western world evokes hope in prospective migrants from developing countries. This can include: hope for a better life, better opportunities for education, health, finance and infrastructure and skill acquisition for themselves, families and future generations. Many of these things are true but it is very important for prospective migrants to know that they cannot be taken for granted.

For economic migrants, the situation and narratives are not the same as it was a decade ago.

No country should allow a situation whereby its citizens travel to another country for low-wage jobs, safety or survival. It is the height of government and societal irresponsibility and failure.

Citizens should leave their countries in order to improve their skills and economic situation compared the situation in their home countries. However, most governments and societies have chosen the path of irresponsibility. They have created situations that push their citizens to other countries for inferior situations and the skilled migrants are usually worse off.

Economic migrant has recently become a mostly pejorative term. It no longer carries the same connotation that it did decades ago, at least in the minds of the ordinary citizens of the host countries. The goal should be to ensure that these people are self-sufficient. However, most of them soon deplete their reserves searching for jobs or acquiring additional required training and qualifications before they are integrated into the economic strata of their new country. The resulting consequences on their social, family, psychological and financial lives are better imagined than experienced.

It has become an easy way to avoid discussions on the precarious situations that most of these people find themselves after arriving in their destination countries. It has also allowed policy makers to distract attention from the urgency of their situations which, in some instances, may be worse than that of a refugee or protected persons.

There are many myths about the subject of migration. What are these myths? What is it about them? What are the realities? These and many other issues will be explored in the following section.

MIGRATION MYTHS AND REALITIES

Myth 1

Economic Migrants Leave Their Country for Better Financial Status.

It is my opinion that the lexicon of migration is far behind today's realities. This is because migrants are broadly classified as:

- Economic migrants;
- Family class-seeking to join family and
- Refugees fleeing persecution, war, disasters etc.

Economics migrants are generally understood as people looking for a better financial status.

I have evaluated my own situation and that of others. I have found that many of them do not fall into any of these categories. This is because there was no war, famine or economic hardship for many when they decided to leave their own countries.

Many skilled migrants, entrepreneurs and investors are grouped as economic migrants. However, the term economic migrant may be a misnomer for many, especially in the skilled worker category.

Many were doing well economically in their home countries and did not really expect to do better economically when they got here. Some are even prepared to accept a lesser economic status.

They are under no illusion they were going to fare better economically. In fact, they were aware of the economic and other uncertainties they faced when migrating.

I was very aware of these factors. It took me a great deal of reflection and extensive consultations before deciding to risk the uncertainties of migration.

"No venture, no gain." Migrants are ready to take some risk here and there in the hope of expanding the horizon of opportunities for themselves and future generation.

Behavioral economists would agree that migration could not entirely be driven by the desire to get more financial freedom. There are many other social, psychological and spiritual angles to it. Many individuals have migrated willfully knowing they would have less financial freedom where they are moving. It is a very complex issue. If you dig deep into people's motivations, you will be surprised at how varied they are.

The motivations and attractions for migration are as varied as the migrants themselves.

The attraction for many is the exposure to other ways of life, different way of doing things, skills, education etc. In this world of knowledge based tertiary industrial revolution, many have come so they can quickly acquire the knowledge, skills and human capital development required to compete and remain relevant in their different fields of endeavor. They are also aware of the opportunities that they and their families will be able to take advantage of if they can visit another part of the world or are able to live there permanently or to have unrestricted access. However, most of them do not have any illusions or unreasonable expectation of an automatic financial gain.

Many of these people can be considered to be adventurous and enterprising migrants. This is descriptive of many skilled migrants. Most of them can be said to believe Andre Gide when he said, "Man cannot discover new oceans unless he has the courage to lose sight of the shore".

They move to their new countries looking to experience different human interactions and to have exposure to other cultures and values, to hone and improve their skills and education and to expand their world view. They are not solely motivated by money.

For this reason, I am sometimes bewildered by the assumption that they have all migrated for economic reasons. This is after you have satisfied curiosities you, like many migrants are not refugees. This does not mean that refugee status makes anybody less than another. That subject will be discussed later in this book.

Many migrants are like the biblical "casting of bread upon water" and hoping to find it later. They find fulfillment from the experiment, experience, entrepreneurship and courage consistent with the saying "it is not life that matters but the courage put into it".

We expect to derive satisfaction from the courage that is put into an endeavor and ultimately our life. Achieving one's goals after a courageous decision can be very satisfying and fulfilling.

It is very true that things can go wrong. Many migrants have experienced serious economic and social problems as a result of this undertaking. A negative experience can also be useful because it will serve as a reference point and a lesson to guide others. It can, therefore, result in positive outcomes.

Many people still decide to migrate despite all of the possible problems. There is something innate in humans that they are always seeking "trouble". We are wired to seek out things and to be adventurous.

Sociologists would be in a better position to explain this phenomenon.

In the wake of global racial and religious tension caused by terrorist attacks: race, religion and skin color have unfortunately become important considerations for economic migrants when thinking of where to migrate.

Myth 2

Migrants Steal Jobs of Natives

"Migrant workers are are asset to every country where they bring in their labour says Juan Somavia, the ILO Director General. In fact, most industrial economies would be worse off without the help of migrant workers, and without the injection of new blood the receiving countries will see their population decline even more rapidly".[4]

There is a common impression that migrants and even skilled migrants steal jobs from citizens and natives of the host country. I do not believe that this is true. It is important to remember that economic migrants are generally allowed to enter a country after the government has decided that there is room for them. How do you invite someone to your house, offer them lunch, and then have your family start complaining that your visitor is stealing their food even to their face? That is very unfair. That is not the appropriate response if you want the visitor to feel welcome. That is an unrealistic expectation. You create an uneven playing ground by telling the visitor to look out for himself by trying to make lunch in your kitchen which he is not familiar with. However, that is what happens when skilled migrants are thought to be stealing jobs. While it is true that their entry into the labor market creates competition for available positions, it does not translate into directly stealing jobs as many people want us to believe. If anything, in this global economy, it promotes healthy competition and excellence that will enable the country to compete better

---

[4] International Labour Organisations, 2008. In search of Decent Work-Migrant Worker's Rights: A Manual for Trade Unionists, section 3, page 46.

in the world economy. It is very easy to see this, since countries who welcome immigrants tend to fair better.

In a free capitalist economy, when more workers come in, adjustments occur in the labor market to create more openings to absorb the new entrants. There may be further adjustments in the placement of these new entrants and some natives in the long run based on their skill sets, education and adaptability. However, this does not actually translate into direct job stealing.

What usually happens is, because there is now a larger supply of labor, the immigrants usually (at least initially) will have to learn the required skills. This frees the citizens and natives to move to the upper level of the labor market strata since most immigrants move into the entry level positions that do not require a lot of skills.

This usually results in higher level positions and wages for the native citizens, and earlier migrants, and at least a foot in the door of entry into the labor market and work force for the immigrant. This leads to expansion in the market and economy of the host country with numerous positive effects.

Many economic migrants are skilled workers. They are not usually drawn to economies where the labor markets are saturated except in the unnatural case of Canada where government continues to attract them, despite the fact that it is very obvious they have taken in too many. As a result, many skilled professionals have gotten stuck and have stagnated. How Canada has been able to obscure this situation and continue to attract prospective economic migrants from all over the world is beyond the comprehension of any rational observer.

Economic factors attract economic migrants to destination countries and that is where their focus generally is. Host countries can be assured that these people can feel the pulse of the economy. The natural law of supply and demand will, to a great extent, eventually regulate movement of economic migrants when the capacity (limit) is reached. If they are still coming, they more often than not still see opportunities in the economy, unless they are manipulated.

The issue of subjectivity is important. The definition of saturated can vary among individuals. It depends on their individual goals and aspirations as well as their experience and background.

Of all the factors of production, humans are the most important and will always be an asset. The host country has free access to this very important factor of production. This may entail some initial expenditure and investment on the part of the host country to help settle migrants and to provide some services. However, there is a net gain over the long term for the host country.

Migration should be a blessing to the host country. There is also a benefit to the source country (at least with the first generation of migrants) through remittances, skills transfer, better international exposure, cultural and value appreciation and integration and promotion of world peace. This, however, depends in a number of factors.

There is currently significant global economic imbalance. The world economy has been dominated by the top one percent. The remaining ninety nine percent must fight for survival. This has resulted in considerable unrest, especially from those who have not been given a fair chance to participate.

However, upon closer examination, there is also unrest and revolution in the western world. These occupy movements are recent examples of these phenomena. These protests differ from one region of the world to the other and from one people to the other. Instead of the capitalists allowing the masses to settle down so that they can determine the root causes of the unrests, they skillfully divert their focus to the effects. As a result, they may never see the real causes, and fail to understand the true situation. The masses need enlightenment for them to appreciate the situation.

The majority in their disadvantaged positions are susceptible to being manipulated by the numerous trouble makers who take advantage of them. They exploit every opportunity to cause disaffection in the world using religion, race and cultural discrimination as excuses to lead people to terrorism, hatred and other forms of intolerance. In most cases, they can easily achieve their aims. Why wouldn't they? The masses most often are not equipped to know better. In general, all they want is a good life for themselves and their loved ones.

The narrative migrants steal jobs of natives is a hypocritical myth. Even on a level playing field, natives or earlier settlers still have lots of advantages over migrants with comparable qualifications. Migrants mostly only find their levels after people they meet in the host country had . Since somebody has to do the job migrants eventually get, the system balances out better with migrants than without.

Is it not hypocritical for corporations to make so many people depend on them for jobs and then go so digital? They are adopting more lean processes every day, yet they talk about increasing unemployment. It doesn't take rocket science to know that one of the undesirable and unintended consequences of lean management is increasing unemployment. This is combined with the fact that many blue collar jobs have disappeared from North America to other parts of the world due to corporations looking for lower labor costs and taxes. Unemployment is a problem that corporations created and which only they can undo. However, they continue to create more of it.

First, they made the small and medium enterprises, family grocery shops, small workshops and trades disappear. Then they absorbed the owners and employees into the corporations or paid them off. They then relocated their factories and sourced their wares and outsourced services from other regions of the world for cheaper labor and taxes. Sourcing products and services abroad kills local businesses. Now corporations are talking about unemployment in a "holier than thou" manner. This is the height of corporate hypocrisy and, in my opinion, is one of the fallouts of neo liberal global economic policy. We cannot always have our cake and eat it too. That is the height of self-deception.

Myth 3

Economic Migrants Lower Wages

Immigration has long served the purpose of a veritable tool to drive national productivity. Capitalism derives a lot of benefit from immigration as a source of labour just as immigration has benefited from capitalism. Since cheaper is a relative term, it can actually be good for the system until a certain tipping aggregate when it could become negative.

While it is true that initially, new immigrants compete for jobs in a country, they are usually the underdogs in this competition. It takes some time before they acquire the skill-sets, nuances and level of comfort to compete favorably for the same positions with native born residents. In the meantime, the labor market naturally expands (adjust) to accommodate new positions as they gradually acquire and assimilate the language, culture and job skills. The most affected are often the previous migrants. They are the ones with comparable skill sets who tend to be either in the low skilled, low wage or entry-level skilled positions, where newcomers usually enter the labor force.

Data have proven that the wage lowering effects are often very marginal and modest. More importantly, as the economy expands, and production and service levels increase, the owners, shareholders, and the economy generally benefits from the economies of scale and the decrease in the cost of labor.

In this way, consumers gain as they begin to pay less, since prices will come down due to larger market. Shareholders and owners who are mostly natives, citizens, and earlier settlers benefit as their dividends and profits go up due to higher production, larger markets, lower wages and all of the other favorable factors resulting from an increase in population.

In addition, the government gets more tax revenues and gross domestic product (GDP), the main dipstick for measuring the economy goes up.

When discussing the lowering of wages and the general decline in the economic well-being of people all around the world, it is sad that people are now forced to put ethnicity, racism, and cultural differences into the discussion of social and economic imbalance, so much that these have now become important considerations for prospective economic migrants.

The capitalists and corporate world have almost successfully diverted our attention away from the "occupy" movements. The one percent and nine-ninety-nine percent narratives have been successfully killed and the populace is now being turned against one another under the guise of racial and religious differences so that the capitalist can continue business as usual.

If there is so much economic imbalance in the world, unbridled capitalism is the major culprit. This is because as we tend towards the extreme in our capitalistic economy, there is little or no help for the weak who are left to their own devices. Many of them are falling through the cracks. However, the capitalists tend to skew the narrative so that people with the least understanding feel that this is the fault of the newcomers.

Myth 4

Migrants Scout for Benefits and are an Economic Burden to Host Country.

This very statement bemuses me. This is because, for the most part, the opposite is true. Most economic migrants have come to better their lots economically. Most of them are natural risk takers, very enterprising, hardworking, positive, and forward-looking. If not, they would not even have left their home country in the first place. The skilled migrant program is especially brilliant because it mostly selects applicants for these traits and attributes by its qualifying criteria.

It is, therefore, antithetical if not absurd to suggest that these people come to the host country to scout for benefits. In fact, research and anecdotal evidence suggest that social benefits are not a primary consideration in their decision to migrate. They are more interested in advancing within the society and the economy and work hard to accomplish that goal.

It is true that many of these individuals enter the host countries as skilled migrants. They are actually wooed by the host country which offers them many opportunities.

It is not logical to say that a group of people takes jobs from you and at the same time call them social benefit scroungers who are a burden to the economy.

If these migrants receive benefits upon their arrival, it is because they are new to the host country. They typically only receive these benefits for a short period of time. In addition, it is a worthwhile investment by the host country because they soon return more in tax payments as they are integrated into the economy and make their own positive contributions.

It is a very prudent investment, which makes economic and political sense for a country to provide the necessary support for new migrants so they can settle in quickly. It usually pays large and quick rewards to the host country.

Host countries that provide support to immigrants soon see increases in their Gross Domestic Product and tax revenues that amount to more than is spent on health, education and the general integration of immigrants.

Astute observers have realized that this is true. Many economic theories and experts also support this. Economic migration is in the best interest of the host country. Most often than not, labor, which is that factor of production difficult to acquire for some countries due to socio - demographic issues, becomes more available and cheaper, markets expand, and productivity in general is enhanced. This drives down the overall cost of production while increasing turnover, unit cost of goods and services, propensity to spend, taxes, gross domestic product, etc.

The net effect is increased revenue for the government to provide services, for shareholders to enjoy, for companies to expand and to the overall growth and development of the host country.

Even the altruistic act of bringing in refugees will most likely turn out to be a wise economic investment if it is well managed. History supports this assertion.

A large number of migrants from China, Vietnam, Africa and Kosovo have at various times migrated into Canada in large numbers. Most of these people and their offspring have settled in over the years and have made enormous contributions to physical, social, demographic, economic and political development of Canada. There are many similar stories in other countries.

By encouraging immigration, societies have historically enhanced healthy competition, transfer and sharing of knowledge, skills, technologies, and values which enhanced prosperity, arts and global understanding.

All classes of migrants can be of great benefit to the host countries, if well managed. Naturally, there will be some bad apples but then the environment they find themselves in the host country may be something to look deeper into. It will not be because they are immigrants but may be due to conditions to which they are exposed.

Social benefits were not created because of migrants but they were developed for citizens and most of the people who use these programs are citizens. No statistics have shown that they are mostly used by migrants.

Myth 5

Migrating to the Western World Makes Life and Financial Freedom Much Easier.

This is debatable. As noted earlier, the prospect of migrating to a developed country creates the hope for a better life and opportunities for the right reasons. There is no linear relationship between migrating to the west and financial freedom. It can be a complex and convoluted process.

The truth is that you need a higher level of effort and skill in the developed world than in the developing world to achieve a comparable set of results/ goals/ objectives/ edge.

It is natural to expect that our abilities and skills will be better honed in the developed world because of the higher level of competition and the stricter standards. The alternative is to settle for less and to remain in the background.

There is no room for mediocrity in most of the western world. As a result, you have to be ready to put in your best. This is good for personal development and an increase in human capital and capacity which is one of the major reasons that people move there.

The lesson to be learned is that you shouldn't deceive yourself in thinking that it is easier to achieve results in the developed world. While you may have better infrastructure, and other supports, competition can be stiff and your competitive edge would be gained by your effort, skill, and mental exertion. You actually would need to put in more effort than you would in the developing world in order to achieve comparative results.

The incentives and opportunities might be there, but you must play your own part to take advantage of them. They are "yours to discover" as they say in Ontario, Canada. These opportunities are there for you to discover.

To do this, you must have invested in yourself in your country of origin. It is what you bring from your home country in terms of skills, finances etc., that you will build on here.

The following is a dialogue that I had with David Mbong, my trainer and senior colleague in Canada.

David: Now that you are licensed, you should be financially okay.

Alaba: Do you think so? I believe that will be relative and very subjective.

David: The reason I say that is because many people believe once they are licensed, their financial worries are over.

Alaba: What is your opinion?

David: Getting licensed is not a guarantee for financial comfort. It might be possible if you own a good practice. But if you think that the hourly wages in this industry will meet all of your needs, you might be dreaming.

Alaba: My thoughts, exactly.

David: Good thinking!

The fact that you are in western world does not guarantee an easy life or financial freedom. The fact you moved to another geographical location, albeit with better "opportunities", does not automatically confer desired success on you or drop them on your laps. No! You still have to discover them. You still have to work for them.

I have been waiting for somebody to show me where and how they pick money on the street or pluck it from trees in Canada. However, my efforts have been to no avail! It is instructive if a professional has not been able to pick money off the street. However, some guys may be smarter and can see what I have not been able to see. You never know. Ha, ha, ha.

Anytime that you are tempted to think people do better financially when they move to the west, pause and think. Could there be a third variable? Could there be any confounding bias? Could it be an instance of selection bias? Could this person have done well even if he had remained at home? These are important questions to answer.

The same natural laws of success still come into play. They include hard work, persistence, continually seeking opportunities and working on self-improvement. There is the need to cultivate productive relationships and interactions with positive and progressive people. Positively seeking and seizing opportunities whenever they present themselves is key.

All of these factors also depend on the individual definition of success.

If you look at the theory of isolation and caging, you would agree that migration increases choices by widening and opening up the migrants' horizon of opportunities.

In this theory, isolation or caging leads to reduced choices. It results in situations where there are no alternatives, to making do with what one has, leading to accepting and making do with what one naturally would not.

Some people don't like being caged in any way. They like breaking barriers. They have global aspirations and thoughts. Migration offers these people an opportunity to increase their choices. However, the migrant must have the vision, courage, resources and resourcefulness to seize these opportunities.

Migrating to Canada in the hope of finding a skilled job is almost becoming a mirage. Leaving your stable, well-paid skilled job in your home country in the hope of getting a job in Canada is very risky.

Migration Myths and Realities

The problem is that people act on stale data and old information. Many people do not have access to current information or choose not to believe what they are told. Others are too optimistic to even investigate current information and therefore act on false, outdated premises. People forget that things have changed over the years. Ever since the last economic meltdown in 2008, things have never been the same and now change very quickly.

The blue-collar jobs that serve as buffer in Canada and much of North America have almost completely disappeared and have moved to other parts of the world where corporations pay lower wages and taxes. As a result, there is great industrial recession in the west. This is the reason for the recent waves of tension. Behind every façade of the reasons that are advanced are poor economic prospects and dwindling discretionary and disposable income due to the industrial recession.

The international value of a barrel of oil has become the dipstick for the global economy. The value for a barrel of oil has declined considerably. This has had a significant recent impact on the Canadian economy. Acting on old information is one of the most dangerous things that you can do.

People don't tell the truth to prospective migrants. People who currently reside here, for the most part, do not tell the truth about the real situation to their friends and relatives who ask them. Using their dishonesty and false sense of pride, they show them beautiful photographs and give them a false impression of an upscale lifestyle and great scenery. In reality, they work their butts off to eke out a basic living. They commonly say of prospective migrants "If you tell them the truth about the real situation, they would not believe you or would think that you do not want them to come and enjoy what you are enjoying." And why and how would they believe you when it contradicts what the government of Canada says on its website? The government is still inviting more skilled workers; by telling them that there are opportunities. So, how would you want them to believe me if I am sounding out a discordant tune? We must not forget that some people don't take advice that conflicts with their illusions and imagination. The new guy comes in, sucks it up and joins the fray, and the cycle continues. However, it is very important to remember that individual cases are different. Despite the many woeful examples, there are still success stories which is what most likely keeps the cycle going.

Much has been said about Canada's high taxes, but there has not been much discussion about the revenues are used for. There are many social welfare programs to take care of people in times of need, good infrastructure etc. The money is being used for many different useful purposes. It is my opinion that we should provide support for the needy and help our neighbors at all times.

This is not to say there are no drawbacks to social welfare programs. This has been well documented but it is better than the alternative of not caring for the weak in the society and the bottom line is to find a compromise. This is one of the things that make Canada tick.

If what you want is increased wealth accumulation, Canada or other western countries may not be able to offer that to you. It is just not one of the goals, aspirations or philosophies of Canadian society.

Myth 6

Migrants are a Security Risk to the Host Country

This is another convenient way of labeling a group of people. Immigration is supposed to foster greater racial, cultural, religious understanding and global peace.

Regular migration should be encouraged and irregular migration discouraged by all and deliberate government policies. However whenever immigration happens irregularly, governments and people of destination countries can still endeavour to make it mutually rewarding by stepping in humanely, knowing fully well the key driver of immigration is still a search for a better life.

Immigration should on the whole bring a positive experience to all stakeholders. Although recent dynamics have some pointers to clash of values and negative tendencies, we can make it ultimately positive if we work together.

When migrants leave their source countries, they actually look forward to assimilating the cultural values and ways of life of their prospective hosts. Most host countries theoretically have deliberate policies to facilitate this immigration. However, the human nature of looking for your "likes" comes into play. Even though government policy is intended to encourage the integration of the migrant, they tend to congregate in communities once they arrive in another country. As a matter of fact, Canada's points system awards points to you if you have someone in Canada who will receive and host you on arrival to the country. This gives an edge to people who have relatives or friends already living in Canada and who are ready to host them. For the most part, the hosts live in a community or immigrant area of the city, and, therefore, the cycle continues. This makes it difficult to become integrated into the society and economy. On the other hand, the citizens who are well established see this group of people as the "others". At a time when migration had not become this rampant, and citizens did not have enough of their "own" to fill their labor and social needs, citizen reached out to the "others". But as soon as he has had a choice due to increased migration, he preferred people that were like his "own".

There is a serious gap and disconnect between official statements and positions on immigration, diversity, inclusiveness and multiculturalism and what actually occurs between many migrants and citizens. A lot still needs to be done about discrimination and stereotyping in many settings. This underscores a need for additional education and enlightenment for a significant proportion of the population. Racial, cultural and religious relations still need to be improved in the western world, especially in Canada. It will require hard work in order to break down barriers for the good of our society.

The more that migrants and citizens interact, the greater the mutual understanding and respect that will develop. Relationships underlie every human interaction. Conversely, interactions underlie every human relationship. There tends to be a positive relationship between these two variables. This is probably the reason that the younger generation and the city dwellers are better in their interaction with citizens and explains why migrants tend to congregate in cities.

There is no official discrimination or alienation from the government which is very comforting.

The migrant, on the other hand, feels comfortable in his environment and social circle. Reaching out to other groups and races becomes a burden and a difficult consideration. Unfortunately, this circle cannot provide much of the assistance and opportunity that he needs to get started in a positive direction. He becomes disaffected by the negative attitudes of the people that he associates with and slips into a cycle of limited opportunity.

In addition to the skills, human capital and whatever else the migrant brings from his home country, other factors influencing his quick integration into society are his contacts and the people that he associates with after his arrival. It will be extremely difficult to be successful if he only associates with other people with limited opportunities.

MIGRATION THE GOOD

Human Capacity Development

We are all naturally attracted to where our human capacity can be developed. Human capacity includes our various individual abilities including: resources, talents, and attributes. The human capital of a society is the aggregate of individual human capacities. It is the sum of the intellect, creativity, imagination, cultural and social enablement in a society, which can be harnessed for the economic, political, cultural and social progress of that society.[5]

Advancement of human capital and by extension of a society on all fronts, therefore, requires a conscious investment in human capacity and human capital development.

The value of a human being and of a society is directly proportional to investment in human capital development. If there is a way to measure investments in human capital development by a society, then we can predict the development of that society. If there is investment in the areas of education, health, moral values and skills acquisition, there is bound to be human capital development, which will inevitably lead to the economic, social and political progress of a nation.

Human beings have amazing innate capabilities. Genetics and the environment are critical factors in the expression and development of these capabilities. Our genetic make-up and what we experience in the environment where we live goes a long way in determining our personalities. It has long been acknowledged that the environment is very critical to human capacity development. The environment is so important

---

[5] Wikipedia, the free encyclopedia; Human Capital, Human Development Index, Life expectancy, Adjusted Life Expectancy (accessed December 15, 2015) https://en.wikipedia.org/wiki/HumanCapital.

that it has been proven to influence the expression of our genes and over several years may modify our genetic make-up. The good news though is that the environment no longer includes only the physical environment. In this information age, the geographical barriers to creating a conducive environment for knowledge and creativity has been reduced. With information technology and new media, you can modify your environment to include resources to spur knowledge, creativity and innovation.

In writing about this, we have to keep in mind that we are focusing on economic migration from less developed to developed economies. Migration also moves in the other direction, but we are focusing on the much larger flow, which is from other parts of the world to the west and especially from Africa to Western Europe and North America.

The social and economic circumstances of many individuals in Africa make migration to Europe and North America to seek better lives irresistible.

The west is the bastion of modern civilization, which is measured and driven by the level of democratic culture, rule of law, human rights protection, infrastructure development, and technological, healthcare and educational advancements. All of these factors interplay with diversity and competition, which fires the basic human instinct for economic survival and advancement. This drives skills development, which is further expressed in the advancement of a society on all fronts.

The presence of an enabling environment perpetuates the continuous improvement of these attributes. There is positive feedback whereby the rewards of these advancements serve to stimulate further search into greater possibilities and on and on it goes.

Developed economies have long realized the direct correlation between human capital development and qualitative growth of a nation. As a result, it has been a major area of investment. This is in contrast to less developed economies where the emphasis has been on physical development (which we do not even do well). This attitude and inclination prevents us from gaining a competitive edge.

It is natural for people to move from an area where their capacities are not being developed to areas where they hope it will be.

When people migrate from less developed countries, their capacities are developed. The first beneficiary of the enhanced capacity is the migrant. This serves as an attraction to continue living in the host country because it is accompanied by other types of positive reinforcement. The environment and host country is the ultimate beneficiary since a well-developed human capacity translates into increased GDP and other variables that enhance the country's ability to compete globally. While developed countries invest in human capacity development and reap the benefits from inventions, innovations etc., the developing countries tend to be "free riders". Nobody respects free riders.

The "Human Development Index" is the United Nation's statistical measure of human development. This encompasses an "education index", income index, and "life expectancy" which is better expressed as "Health Adjusted Life Expectancy".

There is a positive correlation between the Human Development Index and the standard of living in a country. A positive Human Development Index results in good human capital development and the general progress of a nation.

The value of a human being is positively correlated to investment in human resources. If there are human capital investments in the areas of education, health, social skills and values, there is bound to be human capital development, which will inevitably lead to the economic, social and political progress of a nation. The Man 'O' War motto is "Build the man, build the community". This motto is very appropriate.

The western countries where we tend to migrate are the sources of these skills, knowledge, and infrastructural and technological breakthroughs.

These societies have created an enabling environment for this kind of development, so it is natural for people to migrate there from the Third World where most of these things are not obtainable to the developed world where they are.

Over time migrants acquire the necessary set of skills, knowledge, values, and interactions that increase their capacity relative to what they would obtain in the source country. Opportunities to acquire skills in efficient ways and, more importantly, to utilize the acquired skills are more often available in western countries. Developing countries lack key elements to achieve this efficiently.

If a professional migrates from a developing to a developed country, for training, he is able to acquire skills that will place him at a much high level of expertise than what he would be able to achieve in his home country.

If he decides to move back to his home country to practice, he will definitely practice at a higher level of expertise than if he had not earlier left his home country, since he has acquired training and experience from the source.

Many migrants are aware that not much can be changed in their own human capacity development. However. They still choose this path because they hope that their children and future generations will benefit from the move.

On a personal level, calibrating my professional development and confidence level on a scale of 1 to 10 where 1 is the lowest level of global professional confidence and expertise and 10 is the highest, if I was at level 5 in Nigeria, then I am at level 9 in Canada. I believe that this applies to most individuals and professions. The reasons are very obvious.

This means practicing at the cutting edge of one's professional service level. While this does not necessarily translate into higher income, it is very important to the individual's professional and job satisfaction. It allows him to improve his contribution to society. This allows the persons to derive greater satisfaction and fulfillment in their lives. There are also other benefits and improvements that it brings to people and society at large. All of these factors converge to give more meaning to everyone.

I would have loved to be able to go back to my home country to implement all the skills and knowledge that I have acquired. I am sure that it would make some type of difference. This is very much on my mind.

Better Infrastructure and Technology

Electricity, water, housing, good roads, healthcare, food, security etc. are basic things that humans need to live a meaningful life.

They are taken for granted by most people living in the developed countries where the migrants want to be. The issue of paying to enjoy these services is another question. It is usually done by working taxpayers who earn money to pay these services or by the government and other institutions that cover the costs for those who are not able to afford it. The majority of the population is able to enjoy these facilities and services. However, it is necessary to work in order pay for them.

This situation is in sharp contrast to the situation in the source countries. I have witnessed the disappearance of many of these basic services in my country. The first thing that we lost was light, followed by water, roads, public primary schools, public secondary schools and public universities.

There have been efforts to improve these services and institutions. However, the population has lost confidence in the government's ability to do anything about them. As a result, they begin to wonder why they should pay their tariffs. They are not eager to pay because they are not sure that these services will be available.

The weakening and disappearance of our institutions have continued. There are no strong institutions and, therefore, you cannot predict what you will get from any of them. Everything is subjective. It depends on who you meet there. As a result, our society tends to promote "strong men" and not strong institutions. Unfortunately, that is very primitive and retrogressive.

All these things are taken for granted in the countries that migrants target.

The provision of the basic infrastructure and services is essential for successful development. The inability of developing countries to appreciate and comprehend this is very difficult to understand.

In developed countries, you can do whatever you need to do with electricity at any time and any day. If national productivity is the aggregate sum of individual productivity, then it explains why some countries continue to advance while others continue to decline. It is only possible to get out of life, what you put into it. Developing countries need to invest in their infrastructure if they want to improve their national productivity. There is no going around that law of nature.

When I think about life in Lagos, Nigeria and other cities and towns where electricity, water, roads, and other basic infrastructure and technology are still scarce, it makes me wonder why we are surprised at our backwardness. Many of these basic technologies have been around for a long time. Since when did Thomas Edison brought us electric light bulb after being invented by Henry Woodward? How long has it been recognized that good roads and an adequate, clean water supply were indispensable for achieving good health and sanitation?

These basic services have long been recognized as being essential for driving modernization and productivity. They have been taken for granted by many developed countries. However, developing countries still make a big deal about having them. They still form a large chunk of the campaign promises of our politicians and public servants.

You get statements like "I will build roads," "I will provide water" etc. Some governments buy household electric generators instead of building power plants, and instead of building and expanding municipal water plants, they sink boreholes and dig embarrassing wells. Some do not even bother to do anything. As a result, there is a situation where individuals have to provide all these services for themselves. You build your house, dig a well or sink borehole if you can afford it, build a fence around your house and/or hire a security guard, you and your neighbor contribute money to repair your street, drainage, and everything else. You then have to contribute money to hire security guards for the neighborhood watch or you have to watch the street yourselves in rotation. In addition, everybody will have his own household noisy and dirty electric generators that will be blasting away every night with smoke everywhere. The result is a noisy and unhealthy environment. It is also very dangerous since many people that have been asphyxiated in their sleep. This has resulted in the loss of property as well as the loss of the livelihoods of many individuals. The fuels used in the generators have caused many fires and the imported, sub-standard generators malfunction frequently.

Some politicians buy motorcycles for young graduates so that they can become commercial motorcyclists. It is necessary to harness the skills and talents of the bourgeoning human resources that Nigeria is blessed with. There are many obvious, sustainable economic activities that can be done in a more sensible manner. Many of these ideas have resulted in carnage and death. Some governments have contracted their national, state, and local security to militants.

We have had campaigns like "Nigeria, good people, great nation" and we have heard "we have no other country except Nigeria", so let's join hands to salvage "Nigeria." Practical support and offering of tangible and demonstrable assistance and intervention are more effective and enduring in improving the opportunities for our youth and unemployed, than advisements and sloganeering which more often than not offers false hopes.

Our petro-dollars are supposed to provide the funds to support a diversified economy. It is also seen as a means to provide the needed infrastructure and technology. In combination with our abundant human and other natural and intellectual resources, it should have facilitated the development of a strong economy and stable intellectual base. This should have enabled our transition into a developed and competitive economy. It could have enhanced the welfare, productivity and fulfillment of our citizens and future generations. However, the opportunity to exploit these natural resources and to utilize them appropriately has been wasted due to official graft at all levels. The opportunity to build a base that will bring about a strong diversified economy and a bright future is becoming a mirage and wishful thinking. It is a dream which may never become reality since these exhaustive resources are being depleted and graft is festering at all levels.

The world has started talking about climate change and a move to alternate sources of energy with limited or no use of fossils fuels to save our environment. It is only a matter of time before the value derived from our petrol declines with future, dire implications for our country.

If the infrastructure can be improved, people will be able to leave their homes and go to work at any time. Students, and others can wake up anytime, study, and carry out other intellectual activities.

This would result in greater employment and productivity for our society. However, when people have to be indoors as soon as it is dusk and only come out at dawn due to this lack of infrastructure, the reverse is true.

In my opinion, one day in the western world is like three days in developing countries. This means that because of the lack of constant electricity and other infrastructure, one day in Canada is equivalent to three days in Nigeria, one year is like three years, and by extension, sixty years like one hundred and eighty years with productivity and all other things being equal. So why wouldn't productivity be higher in Canada and all other developed countries?

Time is a great equalizer, which we are unable to create. It's a very scarce resource which affects the achievement of many things. Therefore, we must do everything possible to maximize the use of our time if we are to be competitively productive. It requires that we use modern technologies and provide infrastructure for our citizens.

Great countries are being made while people in poor countries are asleep in their homes due to lack of or poor infrastructure. By the time they wake up, they have been left behind. Since this is a cumulative effect, we will remain backward unless we change the status quo and end this retrogressive business as usual.

Infrastructure and technologies impinge directly on other aspects of our lives. This includes other technologies that are indispensable to human development such as education, healthcare, skill acquisition etc.

I consider learning, education and skill acquisition to be means to an end and not the ends in themselves. The end purpose of education is what you use your learning, education or acquired skills to achieve. It is also important in terms of the improvement that you bring to yourself and others as well as society and humanity at large.

In this context, I consider education and learning to be types of infrastructure. They are technologies that bring improvements for humanity and make it more productive.

Effective education and learning are not possible without good infrastructure. Learning, which is the modification of a behavior as a result of experience is also intended to arouse our curiosity and enhance creativity.

Education should make the life of the learner a research in progress. A lifelong inquisitiveness and search for answers to the unending questions ever present with us.

What we learn in school is meant to act as a base for a lifelong learning and to increase and pique our imaginative skills and ability to create. This is because we were created to create. And we should have a system and curriculum that is directed to make us creative.

If what we go to school for is to only learn terminologies and definitions, we have not started to get education and we can never really be creative. Enhancement of creativity should be the essence of education and learning. If what we want to continue to do is to sit back while others take the lead in evolving creative curriculum and learning, then we will only consume those innovations. We will always be free riders and nobody respects free riders.

However, we are not free riders because we pay dearly for our lack of creativity and innovations. We will continue to be laggards whose progress and future will be determined by the so-called developed countries.

Any society that wants to be relevant in this modern world scheme of things where issues are driven by knowledge should be ready to be self-evolving and innovative when it comes to educational curriculum. Our young ones needs the most globally current learning methods, always.

It is not knowledge that matters but the application of knowledge. Knowledge is applied to improve humanity. Of what use is knowledge if it is not applied? Knowledge not applied is no knowledge. The global economy will soon be dictated by knowledge and the movement will continue away from natural resource extraction and industrialization. Any society that claims to invest in knowledge without creating avenues or the environment for its application to more effective human capacity building and societal development is a very bad investor. This concept is elementary.

We pay heavily for our lack of investment in infrastructure, technology and human capacity development. How often have you heard about any breakthrough or innovation from our part of the world despite the many universities, colleges, graduates, professors and other human resources?

By the same token, good healthcare is a technology and a means to an end, which is improved productivity and humanity.

Any honest observer will understand that poor health indices in developing countries like Nigeria is not because of a shortage of physicians or other medical personnel. There are issues with the spatial distribution of health care facilities and personnel which has a negative impact. I remember writing a paper on that topic as part of a case study on the Ondo state of Nigeria.

There is a fair spatial distribution of health facilities; but that is an issue for another day.

Despite these obstacles, our public medical, pharmacy, nursing, physiotherapy etc. schools still manage to produce excellent graduates with a great knowledge base. The problem is that knowledge is only useful to the extent to which it is applied and delivered. The opportunity to apply and deliver knowledge and the environment to make use of this knowledge is what is lacking. What happens when you can't apply and build on that knowledge? You gradually lose it.

A major problem with our healthcare system is diagnostic infrastructure. A great deal of the human body is known and it is so complex that mere description of cases and understanding terminologies and definitions cannot carry us far anymore. In addition, you cannot expect a physician to see every case previously either in training or practice.

The key is in modern diagnostic facilities and the ability for the physician to rule out issues so they can quickly triage a patient for referral to higher or more relevant level of care, if necessary.

Diagnosis is crucial for a clinician or surgeon. Therefore, access to modern diagnostic facilities to complement diagnostic skills is the key to effective healthcare delivery. When diagnosis is not accurate, we cannot even begin to talk about pharmaceutical or nursing care because it will come after diagnosis. The results are the very poor health indices that we have in our nation.

We read about the health issues of our celebrities all the time. We also watch it on television and other media. It is very common to hear a celebrity need some fund to help with treatment of some serious ailments either in the country or abroad but mostly abroad in India, China etc. These are gentlemen and women who have contributed immensely to our society but are so let down by that society. They have become the poster children for our bad healthcare sector. And they are one of the privileged ones relatively as at least help usually comes although may be too little, too late in most cases. Unfortunately, health issues that should be private for citizens have to be broadcast for the whole world before help can come. Millions who are less privileged die without being heard of due to our poor health facilities.

I have a personal story that is relevant. I suffered from stomach upsets and discomfort. They had been mild to moderate in severity, but became so severe that in 2012, I twice ended up in the hospital in Nigeria. My doctors correctly suspected appendicitis based on skilled physical examinations. The symptoms were treated conservatively and everything turned out fine.

In April 2014, I had just taken a job as a staff pharmacist in Medicine Hat, Alberta Canada; about a 3 hour drive from Calgary. I was busy purchasing household items since my family was planning on joining me from Calgary. We were just waiting for the kids to finish their school session in June.

My spouse, Eniola and I were in the car on Macleod Trail in Calgary heading to Canadian Tire, a Canadian department store. As we were driving, I started having severe stomach pain which was more prominent on the right side. My eyes so became blurred and I started seeing double. I felt very nauseous with a very strong urge to vomit. We had the following conversation:

Me: Eniola, I managed to call out.

Eniola: Yes, dear.

Me: We have to go back home.

Eniola: Are we not buying the stuffs again?

Me: No I can't continue; I feel very sick.

Eniola: God! What is the matter?

By this time, I had turned and started driving back home. Fortunately, we had not gone very far from home. It was only about a 5-minute drive.

Me: My stomach. Just generally sick. Very sick.

Eniola: Please let's go straight to the hospital.

At that time, I could no longer afford to talk and my head, eyes and head were already turning and spinning.

I managed to get home. Eniola helped me to our apartment. I managed to enter and immediately started very severe and projectile vomiting. I vomited uncontrollably, like never before. It was crampy and severe vomiting. It was as if my whole intestinal system wanted to force itself out of my mouth.

Eniola: I need to call emergency medical service (EMS).

I waived my hand as a gesture for her not to do that yet. A simple call to EMS would have taken me to the emergency room within minutes. However, I was hoping that the vomiting would stop, so I could clean up the room and myself, and then drive to the hospital.

I was eventually able to do that.

Eniola had to go pick up the kids at their daycare. I told her to stay with them at home and I would update her with a phone call.

Driving when you are nauseous is terrible. The less than 10-minute drive to Rocky View Hospital in Calgary seemed like an eternity. Red lights seemed to stay red forever. I got my car into the first car parking spot, and crawled into the triage area of the reception. By this time, I could no longer speak, and my vision had become so blurred I couldn't see. I was only aware of the pain. I could not sit, stand, nor lie down. I was just listless, and was breathing from my mouth. That was a very horrible situation.

I was quickly examined and given morphine and other things to mitigate the pain. The morphine was magical! I almost told the doctor that I was okay to go home. He laughed and said no.

Doctor: Right now, we don't know what the matter is.

We have to find that out first. Then we will discuss it with our team and make a decision.

Me: Okay.

Doctor: Since we strongly suspect a kidney stone because of the site and the severity described and the fact that you cannot stay still, we will carry out a series of investigations to be sure.

Therefore, a number of tests (imaging and scanning) were carried out very quickly.

Doctor: Hello my friend.

The doctor called out.

Me: Hi doctor.

Doctor: Your tests showed that you have appendicitis.

Me: Hmmm.

"This same appendicitis" I thought.

I had feared the worst.

Doctor: And we have to take it out right away. Are you okay with that?

Me: Sure.

Doctor: We cannot afford not to take it out now. Do you need us to contact your family?

Me: I will do that, doctor.

Doctor: Okay, let them know we are keeping you here for the procedure. We will consult with the surgical team now and let you know.

Me: Sure. Thank you very much doctor.

Doctor: You are very welcome.

I was prepared for the surgery. I understand that I had an exaggerated response to the anesthesia and did not come around as quickly as expected. However, the anesthesiologist and her team were there until everything was stable. There was also aspiration pneumonitis, which they had the resources to handle very well.

These are some of the issues that are taken care of when you are living in a country like Canada. There are infrastructure and services in place for your health needs. They will not fail you in those very things that really matter in life. Healthcare is a very prime and important example in many parts of Canada.

I have had consultations here where I have had to adjust my lifestyle, especially my drinking habits. Lifestyle adjustments were made easier for me because, I was shown the evidence, laboratory results and imaging indicating that it would be very beneficial to me.

What is the take-away here? Are the doctors in Nigeria competent in their clinical skills, and judgment? Yes.

Did they do what they felt would be best in the circumstances? Yes.

Did I get the care that I should have gotten in Nigeria? No.

Was it up to the doctors to make things better? No.

Would the doctors have handled things differently if they have found themselves in a different practice environment like Canada? Yes.

There is only so much a doctor can do if the environment is not conducive and the required facilities, supportive personnel and other determinants of good health care delivery are not present.

How many places in Nigeria can you drive 5 minutes to get to a hospital or be able to call emergency medical services and receive top-class medical attention?

Sometimes it's a matter of life and death and has a serious negative impact on the quality of life if the right things are not done promptly.

In all of these, Canada is far superior to Nigeria. My family members also get top quality healthcare when the need arises.

Nigeria is still grappling with infectious diseases. It is true that diseases can emerge and re-emerge in public health. However, our approach and response is what determines the impacts that it will have on our society. Public health measures to take care of these problems when they happen, should be up to date and ready to be activated.

There was a recent Lassa fever outbreak in some parts of Nigeria. Unfortunately, the approach to public education and mitigation of the impact left much to be desired. It was too rudimentary and primitive. Is this due to knowledge gaps? No. Our public health personnel know exactly what to do and how to do it, if they have the resources. This has been demonstrated in the Ebola outbreak. With the recent help of the Bill and Melinda Gates Foundation, Nigeria has been declared polio free by WHO. However, we still continue to process our foods the way we have done in the past. We continue to spread our grains and cassava, plantain, and yam flour, peelings and chips on rodent infested highways where rodents put inoculum of viruses from their excrement. It is understandable that we will continue to have sporadic cases of Lassa fever or whatever plague there is. It is time that we realized our healthcare is intertwined with education, infrastructure, economics, and ultimately political development. These cannot be separated. Therefore, our most important task is to ensure that we have the right people who can deliver democratic dividends in public offices. Our destinies are in our own hands.

Politicians and other public officials fly to Europe and America to be treated for things as minor as a common cold or headache. What type of society do we have if our citizens have to be flown out of the country when they get sick? In a sane society, these problems are easily taken care of within their healthcare system.

Security

The fences that we mount around our residential and other buildings in Nigeria are legendary. In some cases, the fences are so high you cannot even see the buildings that they are meant to protect. It is a sharp contrast with other areas. These fences are very significant impediments to erosion control, environmental management and renewal. As a result, our settlements lack appeal, aesthetics, and functionality. As a result, we are not able to develop the utilities in our settlements the way that we should. This is a major issue for our urban planners. High fencing is a part of our culture that will remain due to security problems.

There was a time that I had to work in a pharmacy in Red Deer. It is a town about a two-hour drive from Calgary Alberta, where I was living. I left work at about 10:30pm and asked the other pharmacist to recommend a good hotel where I could spend the night. The pharmacist wondered why I didn't consider going back to Calgary, since I could get there by a half hour past midnight. You mean I should drive back to Calgary at this time?

I think you can, she replied. Anyway, I had already planned to spend the night. I will try that next time.

I had thought that idea was crazy and dangerous. But then I came to the realization that my background and experience in Nigeria caused that reaction. I never try to knowingly travel late in Nigeria. It could be really dangerous. I usually spent the night in any town I was in after 7pm. I did that a lot in Nigeria because I used to travel frequently.

In Canada, there is no big deal travelling late at night, if you have to.

Remittances

Migrant remittances have been a major focus of development economics in recent years. They have become a major source of income for people living in migrant source country.

Remittance occur when migrants work in the host/new countries and send some money back to their home country.

Development economists and other interested stakeholders have studied this very important issue. While source countries might have lost human resources and skilled labor in what has long been called brain drain, they gain by migrants returning some of their income to their home country. The host country also gains by the contributions of migrants in their new country. It is, therefore, a win-win situation since the migrant is still attached to the source country. This attachment tends to diminish over time and usually ends with the first generation. Subsequent generations usually have little or no attachment to the source country.

Some individuals have proposed that the new country should pay a percentage of taxes paid by the skilled workers to the source country for a certain amount of time. This is intended to cushion the effect of the source countries' revenue loss, since the skilled workers were paying taxes in their home country and were often trained using source countries' public funds. Therefore, aside from voluntary remittances, the government of the host country should share the taxes paid by these skilled workers who are technically intellectual products. This would be done through an intellectual property tax for a certain number of years. This has been a controversial and challenging issue which no country has been able to address.

Remittances provide the resources to support the education, health, nutrition and overall development of the dependents of the migrant back in the home country. A significant portion of the remittances is also used to build homes, which provide shelter for migrant family members. Many dependents are also helped to start small businesses or to improve the operation of existing businesses. In addition, many of these entrepreneurs or proprietors are women.

Community development programs and projects also benefit since migrants donate to schools, hospitals, community centers and youth development programs. All of these areas are major components of Millennium Development Goals.

As a result of their contributions and their expanded world view based on their western exposure and training, migrants are regarded as important opinion shapers whose views on community issues are respected. They also often form associations and unions that exert influence as political and social pressure groups, working for the best interests of society.

My younger brother Taiwo Victor Ojapinwa, an award winning development economist whose Ph.D. thesis is on Macro Economic Impact of Remittance on Financial Development and Economic Growth of Sub-Sahara Africa is an expert in this area.

Competiveness

Canada's immigration point system for skilled workers is the first of its kind in the world. Under this system, immigrants are allowed to enter based on their score on certain set of criteria. This makes Canada's skilled migrant program a globally competitive undertaking even from the outset. The way the program is designed allows little or no room for partiality.

Canada is very proud of this innovative system. It has been so successful that many countries are said to be studying it in order to adopt it, even the United States of America. This is one of the most important innovations that Canada has successfully demonstrated to the world. I think that Canada deserves a Nobel Prize for this innovation. There are drawbacks to this success that will be discussed later in this book.

Competition brings out the best in an individual, a group and society. The western world generally encourages competition. This brings out the most talented people that their societies have to offer. Everybody strives to the best in whatever they do. Even if you cannot be the best, you try to be your best and you are compensated according to your talent, effort, and contribution to the society.

This is the main way that people are rewarded in western societies. Therefore, other than wishing to win the lottery someday, you know that you will need to work hard to succeed within the system. This will help society and the economy to succeed and will increase productivity thereby facilitating development.

People are able to reach their highest potential in a competitive environment with the knowledge that the western world provides. Our abilities and skills will be maximized in the developed world because of competition and higher standards. Otherwise, this could not be achieved and we would be forced to remain in the background. Therefore, a higher level of effort and skill is needed in the developed world than in the developing world to achieve the same results and goals.

This, in itself, is good for personal development since it increases human capacity development, and societal productivity. On a scale of 1-10, where 1 is the lowest level of professional proficiency and 10 is the highest, if I were on level 5 in Nigeria, I would say that I am on level 9 in Canada and looking at 10. The same applies to most professionals here. This is because there are more opportunities to apply your knowledge and skills if you are lucky to get licensed. The more that you apply your knowledge and skills, the more knowledge and skills you get. In Canada, for the most part, you don't gather knowledge for the sake of it or just get the certificate. The knowledge has to be applicable and must be applied as opposed to what happens in most developing countries. In this way, the system brings out the best for the benefit of society and humanity.

There is a down side to this, though. For example, some people did not come with the adequate skills for the entry level of their profession. Others are not able to enter their desired profession due to stiff competition consequent on an oversupply of talents or because of systematic exclusion. This results in devastating consequences for the migrant and does not enable the host country to benefit from the relationship, as it should do.

The host country must provide support for new migrant so they can settle in quickly and become productive economically in their new country. This will be discussed further in the BAD section.

If you don't want to go to western world to be a factory worker, cleaner, or apple picker, then you better come with a good economic skill or quickly get one upon your arrival.

Cultural Diversity, Multiculturalism and Inclusiveness.

Going by the rhetorics emanating from different parts of the world, whereby separatist and anti-globalization elements seems to be having the ears of some people, even some state actor, Canada stands out as a shining example of how a country can serve as a strong positive force to promote diversity, inclusiveness and multiculturalism, global peace and stability.

This is generally the historical leaning for Canada, although it must be stated it has had and still has its own dots of stereotyping, bias and discrimination which still continues in some settings.

The current prime minister, Justin Trudeau has never been shy to promote the globally inclined ideals and values with renewed vigour. This is repositioning Canada in the scheme of things in global affairs because it happens this is the kind of values the world need the most now, going by contemporary issues facing humanity.

Many around the world love Canada for this. Many Canadians too are mostly pleased and happy with their prime minister and can't be prouder of him.

There is no doubt there are still some rough edges in the relationship between ethnic groups in Canada. A great deal of work still needs to be done. The good thing is conversation and action around this are ongoing and continuos. Obvious progress are being made.

This is why despite the gloom and doom pervasive in different parts of the world, Canada still represents an example of a place where there is hope of improved racial and ethnic relationship being facilitated by the state and the people themselves.

Many countries around the world are seeing Canada as a model and looking to learn from her. As Canada continues to to build on these values and tendencies, it can only continue to be a positive force and influence in driving global inclusiveness, stability and peace.

Western countries are very magnetic to prospective economic migrants. People come from every part of the world to seek a better life for themselves and future generations. These countries are, therefore, melting pots for different cultures, values, and languages. As a result, people gain insight into life in other parts of the world. There are enormous advantages in giving people a broader view of the world and a better understanding of other peoples' backgrounds than they would ordinarily have if they had remained in the usually relatively homogenous cultural environment of their home countries. This heterogeneity, multiculturalism, and diversity promote and enhance an individual's interpersonal and social skills, tolerance, and sense of community and world peace.

Migrants usually try hard to adopt the values and to become integrated into the way of life of their new country. However, they still have the freedom to use their language, culture and religion in their individual homes, community groups and other times that they come together.

A society where cultures and values meet and mix is the best opportunity for training, learning, and practicing tolerance, accommodation, understanding, compromise, and peaceful healthy co-existence. This type of setting can also foster healthy competition.

Canada takes pride in its cultural, religious, racial and sexual orientation diversity. It also promotes its inclusiveness.

Canada is a country with a mixture of values, cultures, religions and languages. Of all the most advanced global economies, Canada has the highest percentage of foreign-born citizens, since approximately twenty percent of Canadians are foreign born. Migration is critical for Canada's formative history, demography and an important aspect of its future demographic development. Foreign-born immigrants are most commonly located in the cities and urban areas of Toronto, Montreal, Vancouver, Calgary, and Edmonton in the large provinces of Ontario, Quebec, British Columbia and Alberta.

Canada has done a good job of promoting inclusiveness. It has instituted deliberate policies to protect the interests of migrants, visible minorities and diverse groups. Compared to similar western countries, Canada has done well. In terms of employment and job prospects, there is a diverse culture where employers strive to represent diversity and multiculturalism in their employment policies. Migrants are even given equal opportunities in public service positions epitomized by the current Justin

Trudeau's government where immigrants occupy a number of key ministerial positions.

Bill Clinton and other world figures have attested to this at different times. Whether the president or citizen of a country is competent to tell the story of another country, is the question. He can only base his views on what he has heard and limited exposure which will be superficial. As a citizen, I agree that Canada stands far above other countries in this regard.

However, there are still some gaps and disconnects between official positions and individual, racial, religious and cultural interactions. As a result, citizen enlightenment and education still needs to be done in many areas.

Skill and Technology Transfer

Many skilled migrants come to western and developed economies to develop their skills. They are able to get training and practice in this part of the world. They are, therefore, able to practice at the competitive edge of their profession. This western exposure, with the associated knowledge and training is mobile and transferable.

If the migrant ever decides to move back to his home country, he would definitely practice at higher level of expertise due to his exposure and experience, knowledge, skill, and practice. Returning migrants have much to offer their home countries. They also possess the social and capital capacity that is required to develop the service industry and a bourgeoning middle class, which is the bastion of sustainable development.

Better Political Culture, Leadership, Follower Ship and Government.

There is a lot about the present political culture, leadership and follower ship in Canada that many countries around the world have to emulate.

Looking at the aggregates of these, many would rather be in this great country than anywhere else in the world.

The core business or responsibility of government should be to ensure the welfare of its citizens. A society can be described in terms of its leadership and followers. In an organized society, to ensure orderliness, a group of people is entrusted with power in whatever form the society decides. This group of people controls the affairs of the society.

For a harmonious and balanced system to result from this relationship, everyone must have their prescribed roles and responsibilities. They should also play their defined roles. In a normal situation, leaders make decisions on which way to follow and walk the talk in order to set good examples for followers.

An uninformed community cannot be democratic. I agree that informed followers are very fundamental and crucial to good leadership. However, they must demand accountability. In order to do this, they must be informed. Good leadership within a country comes from the persistent demand for it from the people. People might be said to deserve the kind of leadership that they get.

In a political system, what matters most is public opinion. As public opinion changes, leaders and politicians will want to protect their jobs and adjust their policies to meet the public interest. Those who refuse to adjust should be smart enough to know it will be just a matter of time before public opinion will sweep them away so that the natural course is restored.

Unfavorable conditions (perceived or real) in the countries of origin is one of the major causes of migration to host countries. Poor leadership and governance in the country of origin is often the cause of these unfavorable conditions. Correcting this poor leadership in order to reduce migration is very difficult, which few countries or organizations are ready to confront and tackle. This is even more difficult because migration in many ways fulfills the goals and aspirations of the migrant. At the same time, it meets the needs of destination countries as a supply of labor, a means of demographic expansion and a means to increase productivity.

The quality of leadership in the developing countries is very poor. Considerable effort and financial investment have gone into making developing countries self-sustaining.

The process of getting into leadership positions in these countries does not usually result in the best person being selected for the job. The selection process usually has inconsistencies, irregularities and lack of transparency. This results in unqualified individuals being selected for leadership positions. More qualified individuals tend to stay away due to irregularities, finances, insecurity etc.

For this reason, the first step to be taken is to ensure that the electoral processes are as transparent as possible. This is essential in order to achieve democracy and good leadership in these countries.

I believe that our society must find a way to get the right people to enter politics. These individuals must have personalities that are innovative, selfless, competitive, hardworking, knowledgeable, accommodating, decisive and visionary. This is very different from the types of politicians that we have now. Most developing economies attained political independence several decades ago. However, the independence of the population of a country is not guaranteed by pronouncements, sloganeering or writing on a piece of paper. This is just self-deception and delusion.

A people of a country get independence by working for it. In addition, the people must be able to demonstrate their independence. In most cases, however, there is only talk of independence when it is convenient and suits our purpose. Has Africa, for example, been truly independent since we got self-rule?

Political independence should not be without other forms of independence. Do we want to be politically independent without working? What the Nigerian political class has been doing is enjoying the perks of political leadership without taking on the responsibilities that is attached to it. This includes the need to enhance the welfare of their citizens.

Nigeria continues to be an appendage to western countries and depends on them for the most of their basic needs. The political leadership has not demonstrated the patriotism that is necessary to move us forward. Instead, corruption and ineptitude have been the order of the day. This has significantly slowed our political and economic development despite having been politically independent for almost six decades.

Independence should benefit everyone but the political class is using it for their own selfish and myopic political gain. An example is the Ebola virus, where we immediately sought help from the western world. It took the western world giving us a tap before we even acknowledged that our girls were being kidnapped. For minor medical issues, our leaders are on the next flight to Europe and America. There is also medication, infrastructure and even food that must be imported from western and other countries.

Millions of students are sent abroad by government, parents and other sponsors. They pay very expensive tuition not to study science and technology courses which are lacking in Nigeria, but for courses in the humanities and business.

How does a country justify such a senseless capital flight in this information and technology age?

We even had sent our legislators abroad for them to learn the art of legislation. All these are happening after almost six decades after independence. What then is the meaning of our independence if by now we haven't developed our own legislative template? Some argue that military upheavals are responsible but I don't accept that argument. That is so much for the political independence of a country.

We understand that a country cannot really be totally independent in this modern neo-liberal world. It is my opinion that we are all interdependent. Global collaboration is recommended in this modern world, but we should at least be independent in these basic things.

In the Nigerian example, our petro-dollars were supposed to have been able to help develop a diversified economy. It was supposed to have been a fertile land and the harbinger of a strong economy. The petrodollars should have been used for an industrial revolution that would have made us economically competitive. Perhaps this would have reduced the number of individuals who wanted to migrate to the western world for economic reasons.

We have missed the opportunity to exploit oil as a base on which to diversify our economy with a solid infrastructure. What is going to happen when these exhaustible resources are depleted?

The world is now talking about climate change and looking for alternative energy sources such as renewable energy. It is time to get our act together as a country and to be futuristic in our policies. We need to act fast and be innovative in our search for alternative sources of revenue before we find ourselves in direr economic conditions than we are right now.

The world is talking about climate change and a reduction in carbon emission. It is important for a country like Nigeria to look inwards and to be proactive in searching for alternative sources of revenue other than petrol exports. It is only a matter of time before carbon based fossil fuels are replaced by non-carbon sources like wind, solar, hydro and other renewable energy sources.

There are arguments the west is talking about reducing global carbon emission after they have gone past their own industrial revolution and they are now investing in knowledge based industries, IT, high technology and other tertiary industries. That emerging industrial economies such as India, China and some African economies will be hurt the most by this new direction in global energy and environmental policies.

However, this argument is simplistic and does not recognize the contributions and sacrifices that have been made by the western world led by the United States of America. These efforts will go a long way in sustaining the earth and to save the earth. With such strong scientific data in favor of this change in energy sources, it is prudent to start acting now.

No country should make its citizens migrate to another country for survival jobs and not to talk about declaring them to be refugees. It is the height of governmental and societal irresponsibility.

Citizens should leave their countries in order to improve their skills and economic status compared to their home country. However, the reverse has been the case for many migrants in recent years. There are many countries whose governments are not in tune with global policy directions. This pushes their citizens into very difficult situations. Many migrants, including many professionals, turn out to be worse off with migration.

Government Social and Community Support for the Financially, Physically, and Mentally Handicapped.

The measure of a good government or a just society is how much it protects the interests of the weak in the society. To a very large extent, Canada is a socially just society. They support the weak in their country. Just as a chain is only as strong as its weakest link, a society is only as strong as the weakest in the society.

There are various programs and support for the financially, physically, and mentally handicapped. Even in the design of their public and private buildings, there is consideration for the mobility of the physically handicapped. This is a very thoughtful society. I have seen many people who had earlier relocated back to their home countries who move back to Canada for the sole fact that there are programs to support family members with special needs.

This humane policy and culture is one of the things that makes Canada great. There is no better feeling than knowing that your government and people have your back and want to be the best for you.

MIGRATION THE BAD

Non-Integration

Delayed or non-integration into the economy and social structure results in dissatisfaction, disaffection, deviant social tendencies and a sense of non-inclusion and not being wanted. It is similar to being invited to a home, and when you get there, you discover that you cannot relate to or sit down with your host but must stay with the people that you came with. As a result, you are on your own. This may not be unexpected given how much individualism has been promoted in North America.

This creates a situation where theories of racism, discrimination, neglect and non-inclusion will have a receptive audience.

Throughout the western world, immigrants congregate in particular areas. However, some of these individuals are able to break this pattern through their skills, personalities, determination and good fortune. However, they soon find out that although they might have relocated geographically, their hearts and minds still go back to where their "likes" are. Some individuals can choose to ignore this and seek to become fully integrated into society. The choice is theirs.

It has been argued that immigrants do not integrate or assimilate into society. However, these assertions are made without taking the time to examine and analyze the forces that migrants must contend with. In order to gain a better understanding of the situation, it is necessary to take a broader perspective. The question that should be asked is: Why would a migrant whose mind and heart was open enough to leave his home country and travel thousands of kilometers in the hope of better opportunities, a new environment and new social contacts not want to integrate in the new community that he has dreamed about and consciously moved into? That does not make sense.

If you could examine the mind and heart of the prospective immigrant when he was leaving his home country, you would find that he would be looking forward to new friendships and associations with his hosts and native citizens. However, he is usually very disappointed, since his best contacts will remain people from his home country.

While it is natural for them to settle first in an area where they have contacts, they want to become integrated with their new hosts in general and to feel at home. This is only possible if your hosts make you feel welcome.

Therefore, Canada, instead of having a Minister of Citizenship and Immigration, should have Minister of Citizenship, Immigration and Integration. The integration part is critical for a country that has so much immigration. What is the purpose of immigration if migrants are not consciously integrated by more deliberate government policies and actions than we currently have? This is food for thought for the Canadian government.

Once you have developed a sense of not being welcomed, the tendency is to look for something familiar such as your own people. Many people start feeling homesick immediately after they get here because of the social alienation in their new country.

This is one of the major reasons why immigrants congregate and create their own replica of their home country for themselves in their new country. They do not feel welcomed for the most part.

It, therefore, means that the host needs to reach out to them more. Otherwise, the migrant loses out on their economic and social opportunities and begin to feel like they are being discriminated against. The lack of economic and social opportunities reduces their access to education and employment. This results in poverty, crime, disease, poor intellect, racial and religious tension and many other societal ills which turns cyclical and becomes everybody's headache.

Therefore, although it is very convenient for us to point to a pattern of security issues and crimes in urban areas with large immigrant populations, it is necessary to evaluate the situation objectively. The majority of these problems are due to the lack of opportunities for the migrant population.

There are numerous examples where the people with the most social problems are the natives. The native population has been dominated by the early migrants politically, economically and culturally. These are the same people who point to the natives as security risks and crime mongers. Examples of this practice are native Africans in South Africa and Native Americans in North America. The common denominator is the lack of opportunities.

If you are moving to another country, it is very important do everything within you power to become economically productive as soon as possible when you get there. You should try not to be on social services if possible or not longer than necessary if you have to. This will allow you to raise your head high when some uninformed person accuses immigrants of living on social services. Over time these feelings and the stereotyping will decrease. If this is done social benefits will be limited to emergency situations such for refugees and asylum seekers. However, it still may be more convenient to label migrants as social support scroungers. However, you should not let the negative labeling prevent you from seeking government help when you have to because that is why it was set up, to help the weak.

It is important to get integrated and assimilated into your new country in every possible way. This should be done while maintaining your original culture as much as possible. This should be done by cultivating new friends and associations, wherever possible. It is also crucial to learn the language and local customs as quickly as you can and to get involved in your community.

71

The idea of immigrants congregating and creating an environment similar to their own country can only carry us so far. It can result in a very negative situation if it is carried too far.

It is essential to prepare and position yourself so that you will be useful to your new country. If you don't, it is likely to result in discontent, dissatisfaction and lack of fulfillment. This breeds feelings of discrimination and other negative emotions.

It is recognized that this is very difficult to do. If you have tried your best as a skilled migrant and economic integration and assimilation prove to be unattainable, unachievable or not in sight, then it is time to review or change your strategy. Consider the possibility of returning to your home country or another place where you know that you stand a better chance. In many cases, skilled workers can still pick up the pieces that they left it in their home countries.

It is important that every migrant has a clear, written exit strategy. If the migration experiment (it should be an experiment until proven to be successful) does not work out, you can use your exit strategy script for your return to your home country.

There is no point in overextending your welcome if you are not going to succeed. If the migrant stays in the host country without full integration into the economy and society, it will breed a dissatisfied and disgruntled generation that poses security and other risks to society. This is because once an immigrant finds it difficult to integrate in all areas, it negatively affects his or her offspring. It will result in a cyclic pattern of being a disadvantaged generation that lacks access to education, skills, social interactions and other opportunities.

A classic example is in the United States of America. Since the abolition of slavery, blacks have not been given fair opportunities. As a result, system discrimination continues.

This situation breeds hatred, dissatisfaction and feelings of discrimination and non-inclusion which leads to very serious deviant behaviors and social liabilities.

This is why it is important that host countries, citizens, immigrants and other stakeholders all play active roles in quick integration and economic and social productivity of immigrants. We all have much to gain by doing that and much to lose by doing otherwise.

Poor Skilled Job Prospects

The quest for better job opportunities, wages and satisfaction are among the major drivers of economic migration and especially for skilled workers. Canada has had a very successful skilled migration program with many professionals moving in and able to fulfill their professional financial dreams.

However, the global economics crisis of 2008-2009, even though did not officially affect Canada, seems to have changed the situation.

The skilled migrant program has been so successful that a glut of professionals has developed in the Canadian labor market. Because of the way that the points system has been handled, this ingenious and innovative policy is having a negative effect and a backlash on the image of the economy and the fortunes of the country. Many skilled workers have moved into the country, only to find themselves destitute.

The economic policies of western countries and the global economy have been neo-liberal for some time. Many jobs have been outsourced to developing countries with lower wages. With the end of the industrial revolution and the growth of the services, knowledge, and IT industry, many western labor markets no longer generate many unskilled and low skilled positions which served as entry points for new skilled and unskilled migrants into the labor market. The blue-collar jobs have almost disappeared.

This creates competition between the citizens and the new migrants. In this situation, the migrant will either find himself in an unskilled or low skilled position or will have to navigate the difficult path of getting his education and skills recognized. He may have to get completely new skills and training in order to qualify for a skilled or semi-skilled position.

In many cases, doctors are retraining to become nurses. In addition, engineers, accountants, business managers and Ph.D. holders are retraining. Many of them would be lucky to become registered nurses.

This places many skilled migrants in an economic and career progression disadvantage. As a result, many of them become stagnated.

Skilled workers are lured to Canada with the promise of a better life. They are also given the impression they will be able to get established quickly. Whether, this happens is not dependent on whether or not the skilled migrant works hard or not. It depends on a number of other factors that are not predictable.

The situation for skilled migrants is very different than it was a decade ago. The point system takes into consideration education, job experience, age, social ties, financial ability, etc. Points are awarded to each of these factors. If you earn the required number of points, you are considered to be qualified. It is then necessary to go through medical and security checks in order to become a skilled migrant with permanent residence status on arriving in Canada.

The problem starts when the skilled migrant arrives in Canada and discovers that his foreign education and experience does not count! This is a setback for the skilled migrant. The question is why did your credentials qualify to immigrate as a skilled migrant but not recognized or even get you an entry level or training position in you field? In most cases, you will not even get the lowest or support position in your field, not to mention training positions.

It is unreasonable to expect that the Canadian Immigration Commission be the credentials and knowledge screening body for foreign trained professionals for admission into a professional practice. That is one of the mandates of the various professional regulatory bodies. The question is, if all of the skilled migrant's training and experience is suddenly irrelevant, to the point of not even able to get a supportive role, what are they supposed to do?

I am very sure that if most skilled workers knew this before coming to Canada, many of them would have planned their migration process differently. Nothing in the information provided to them by Canadian Immigration Commission suggests the level of difficulties that they experience. Skilled workers should do their own due diligence and private investigations of their career prospects when migrating into a new country. The considerable hype about the numerous prospects in Canada will require examination and research by the prospective migrant.

A pharmacist with many years of experience is not allowed to work as a pharmacy assistant or even get a volunteer position in a pharmacy! Unfortunately, most skilled migrants in regulated industries have worked for a long time in their professions and are not able to get placed. Other industries won't take them because they don't have experience in that field. This puts the skilled professional between a hard rock and a hard place.

This large group of people including doctors, pharmacists, engineers, nurses, teachers, accountants, bankers etc. are now forced to take low skill or unskilled jobs as factory workers, daycare workers, cleaners, cashiers, grocery store clerks, pizza delivery people, and the lucky ones, taxi drivers. This can be very frustrating. This situation has made many see the Canadian immigration system as dishonest or at the least misleading.

Many have come to Canada as doctors, pharmacists, lawyers, bankers, etc. but have found themselves work as security guards, factory workers or cashiers. In many cases, it does not matter whether you are brilliant or not.

Regardless of previous qualifications, it is extremely difficult to get a skilled job in Canada without first going to school here.

The top-bottom approach of the government in determining the number of skilled professionals to bring in apparently has been done without adequate consultation and coordination with prospective employers and professional regulatory bodies. This should be a bottom-top approach where the data and statistics come from employers and professional regulatory bodies.

However, the current arrangement seems to work for the employers because it is creating a buyer's market for them where there is abundance of workers to choose from. This gives them the negotiating advantage to drive down wages. This may be good for employers but not for the image of the country.

Due to the capitalist mindset of most employers, business owners, and the corporate world, the oversight function from government must be persistent and strong.

Much has been said about Canada luring professionals here only to systematically place them in unskilled positions. This is a policy, procedure and strategy failure which should change in the interest of the image of the country.

I have an idea for the different professional bodies since these issues have reached a crisis and tipping point in some professions. Let prospective skilled migrants go through their evaluating and qualifying processes to a certain level before leaving their home countries. By whatever means or arrangement necessary, let them go through the accreditation process to a level to which they will most probably qualify when they land before coming in.

This way, we will avoid producing disgruntled professionals who are "lured" out of their various countries to come for skilled jobs (at least that is the impression or expectation), only to find themselves as cleaners, security guards, and factory workers.

This is spiritually, psychologically, politically, strategically and the morally proper thing to do. It would not have been a problem if it were only a few instances. However, this is an enormous problem that must be nipped in the bud. If not, we will continue to breed dissatisfied persons and generations who will continue to feel disgruntled for being deceived into coming here.

I have seen a number of Ph.D. holders who move to Canada with the intention of finding middle level jobs only to be disappointed when there are no spots for them.

Migrants who had been lecturers in their countries would be considered for high school teaching jobs if they would do a series of training classes. This takes a number of years. If you took the training it does not automatically mean you would be considered. For some migrants, apart from the issue of few available spots, accent is an issue. How do you employ a foreign tutor with a strong accent to teach elementary and high school students who would end up not understanding him or her due to their accent?

A conversation about this topic came up between myself and my friend and neighbour Bonaventure Agbonton. We were sitting in the balcony at the back of the house after work, one evening. He has a Ph.D. in entomology from Germany, and was working in a research institute after coming to Canada as a skilled immigrant.

Alaba: How was work today?

Bonaventure: Fine, I can't complain.

Alaba: Yes. There is always something to make work interesting if we want to make it.

Bonaventure: I may not be doing this for a long time more though.

Alaba: Are you planning a career move?

Bonaventure: I have to. For one, I am on contract here. I am on two-year contract, which will end in a couple of months from now.

Alaba: So, they are not going to renew the contract?

Bonaventure: Not sure yet. They have a way of keeping you in suspense. You would have thought that by now, I should be clear if it is going to be renewed or not.

Alaba: Nobody likes a prolonged suspense.

Bonaventure: Secondly, I am kind of underemployed here. The impression was with my qualifications and skills; one would have the prospect of becoming a staff member with the prospect of career progression.

Alaba: Have you tried to apply to higher positions?

Bonaventure: Vacancies are few and far between. The one or two that are advertised, you are told you are overqualified. These are positions that are higher than what I hold now, but they employ first-degree holders. They keep you where you are with the excuse that you are overqualified!

Alaba: So it is a case of your higher qualification working against you.

Bonaventure: Exactly.

Alaba: I hear that a lot. That is a very common story and scenario.

Bonaventure: Very common.

Alaba: There is one of my colleagues at work whose husband had lectured for ages before moving here. He was also in one of these research institutes more or less like a technician. There was no job satisfaction nor career progression prospects. His issue has also been over qualifications for the position he had applied to.

Bonaventure: I tell you.

Alaba: The issue is that Canada definitely brought in many more skilled workers than they can accommodate.

Bonaventure: Exactly.

Alaba: So people come here to be demoted.

Bonaventure: Yes, and that is if they ever get a position where they are trained or any skilled job at all.

Alaba: Why can't Canada match their needs with the intake process as much as possible so that people's careers are not decimated or truncated just because they moved to Canada as skilled workers?

Bonaventure: I don't know. These guys doing the intake are not very sensible.

Alaba: People get here to discover they have boarded a "one chance" taxi. The majority of them find themselves in the middle of nowhere as far as career progression or even any skilled career is concerned. May be Canada has a lot of room for low skilled workers but not for skilled migrants.

The demand is not close to the rate that they bring them in.

Bonaventure: Truth be told. Many people come here and become very disillusioned. There is too much hype about Canada's capacity to absorb skilled migrants.

Alaba: I agree. Many people are being shortchanged, career wise.

Bonaventure: When you have been shortchanged career wise just because the whole picture was not painted to you from the outset, what do you do?

Alaba: Then you have to do a structural reset. You have to review your plan and put your destiny in your own hands. Like I usually say, if you are entering anywhere, you need to have an exit strategy beforehand so that when the going gets unreasonable, you can get out.

Bonaventure: That is exactly what I am going to do.

Alaba: What do you have up your sleeve?

Bonaventure: I have started sending my resume all over the world. In fact, I have 3 interviews scheduled for next month. I have one each in Germany, the United States, and South Africa. All of them have better prospects.

Alaba: That's great!

Bonaventure: A big one with the United Nations that may be locating me in Nigeria to manage a project across West Africa is coming up too. I will opt for that if I am offered that job.

Alaba: Who wouldn't?

Bonaventure: I hope to complete my citizenship processes and get my Canadian citizenship very soon before the offers start rolling in, so I would not need to be coming back and forth because of that.

Alaba: You are highly encouraged brother.

Bonaventure: I will move back to West Africa once I get the job.

He did just that because he got the job. He has been very happy ever since with that decision.

Alaba: In all these cases, Canada as a country loses a lot. I was looking at a write-up recently where it was stated that by not recognizing foreign credentials of skilled migrants, Canada loses a lot economically. Some have placed a dollar value of tens on billions of dollars annual loss to the Canadian economy due to this.

Bonaventure: That is a big loss to the economy. The bigger problem, however, is the induced poverty among these skilled migrants. The situation leaves very much to be desired.

Alaba: You are right. There is so much difficulty in getting foreign credentials recognized. Added to the difficulty of securing jobs and career advancement for skilled migrants, poverty and frustration are the natural consequences.

Bonaventure: Why is Canada still bringing in more skilled workers?

Alaba: You can ask that question again.

Augustus: And in all they are not changing their approach or are still doing same thing and calling it another name.

Alaba: Yes.

Bonaventure: What an opportunity Canada is losing!

Many skilled workers end up in dead end jobs since they cannot afford to continue acquiring the ever changing required skills and re-certifications when the bills start rolling in. They need to work to pay the bills. Most of them have families, so between paying bills and taking care of their families, it becomes very difficult to advance their qualifications and as a result, they are hooked and never integrate skill and profession wise.

Some are lucky enough and are able to brave the odds and fully integrate themselves economically.

Many youngsters come to Canada to study. They are either self-sponsored or sponsored by parents, governments, and other organizations.

Canada is a very good place to receive training, education and skills. It is a country where you will be trained to practice at the cutting edge of your profession, discipline and trade. They have a globally competitive knowledge and technology industry so it is very smart to get trained here if you want to be globally competitive.

I came across Kola. He is a young Nigerian. He moved to Canada after receiving a first degree in transport management. I met him in the library.

Alaba: Hello, young man.

Kola: Hi.

Alaba: How are your studies going?

Kola: They are going on. I am writing a certification exam next week.

Alaba: And what is that about?

Kola: Diploma certificate in project management.

Alaba: That is a good one. What is your background?

Kola: Transport management. I had my first degree in Nigeria and my master's degree in Canada.

Alaba: That's cool. Are you going for a Ph.D.?

Kola: That would have been desirable but you know here you sometimes have to wait a long time to get Ph.D. offers.

Alaba: Yes, I know.

Kola: Plus, the cost! It can be very expensive unless you get sponsorship. Student loans might be available in some instances, but they can be very huge and become a great burden later.

Alaba: Like somebody said, "student loans are like HPV, once you get it, it stays with you for life."

Kola: Ha ha haa. That's extreme!

Alaba: Coming to your case, unless you get a teaching position or job with good remuneration when you finish.

Kola: And that can be a long shot. There are so many Ph.D. graduates looking for positions now. I won't even try that for now.

Alaba: That's tough.

Kola: Ph.D. may even be disadvantageous because then you are branded "over-qualified" when you apply for jobs.

Alaba: I've heard that. Too much qualification often can be disadvantageous in the industries.

Kola: Who wants to employ Ph.D. holders in the industries?

Alaba: They will naturally think you will be too "bookish" which is not necessarily so. Ph.D. only means you have expertise in a main area which can be very good and an invaluable addition to a company.

Kola: That can be a tough sell to many companies and even governments.

Alaba: So what's your plan?

Kola: After this project management certificate, I will start looking for job while I complete my MBA, which I have started.

Alaba: You are working on an MBA too?

Kola: Yes, that is the way it is here. You continue acquiring certificates until you fit into a good position one day.

Alaba: Would that not put you at the risk of being considered over-qualified which will ironically reduce your chance of getting a good job?

Kola: What can I do?

He asked looking as if he suddenly realized that possibility.

"But what do I do? That is why we tend to acquire our credentials. Acquiring qualifications laterally and not vertically, if you know what I mean.

Alaba: I think I know. Instead of moving from first degree to masters, Ph.D., post-doctoral and others, you do first degree, masters and then acquire different certifications like project management, business administration, cost management, personal management etc.

Kola: Exactly.

Alaba: That will make you become a perpetual student.

Kola: Something like that.

Alaba: It will also help the market for the ever booming post-secondary education industry here.

Methinks, these trainings and certifications were originally designed to be acquired on the job before some smart educational industry experts thought of making them distinct courses. There is nothing bad in getting these from the scratch though.

Kola: Bros! You are a troubleshooter o. What do you think is happening before. Lots of people send their wards here from different countries for all these trainings and skills. Most of these people in a bid to stay behind and most often with the backing of their people at home continue to acquire more credentials in the hope of these will make them integrate economically here.

Alaba: Uhmmm

Kola: In the process they provide good market and returns for the educational and training industry here, which makes these institutions better like a positive feedback mechanism.

Alaba: Naturally!

Kola: The result is that the industry gets better and better. Too many stay behind however and so not enough job positions to absorb them as they compete with skilled migrants and others.

Alaba: Seriously!

Kola: The result is you find highly educated folks in semi-skilled and un-skilled jobs all over the place.

Alaba: I have a question for you.

Kola: What is it?

Alaba: How about moving to other parts of the world after acquiring all your certificates?

Kola: Somebody has suggested that.

Alaba: Or even moving back to Nigeria, or somewhere in West Africa. We need your skills there. Nigeria is trying to revive her rail transportation, more investment are going to roads, sea and air transportation. That is a developing industry in Nigeria and that is where I think you will be more useful.

Kola: Bros, I don't know why we find it so difficult to think along that line once we get here. There is almost always a pressure to remain here.

Alaba: That is because of the poor leadership and in Nigeria. Things are beginning to change however, and it is good to key in for our good and for the good of our place of birth.

Kola: Correct!

Alaba: What I mean is, those who come here to acquire western education, skills and training and then go back home to work and apply their skills get a better deal as far as getting a good and relevant job, career prospect, and even financial freedom and job satisfaction is concerned.

Kola: I think you are right. That is the trend in recent times. Just that most of us find it difficult to brave the move to go back home even though the sincere reality is most are finding things very tough here.

Alaba: That right?

Kola: How about you sir?

He asked, kind of mischievously.

Alaba: Don't you forget I came in here as skilled worker and not as a student like you. I replied in a taunting joking manner.

And I am here with my family, unlike you, who have not even started thinking about marriage, although you are a small boy.

Kola: Bros. that is another complex issue. Don't let's go there for now.

Alaba: But you can't run away from it if you have to do it. You still have to tackle it.

Kola: Yes, but that is a very knotty issue for us immigrant boys. Not a lot to choose from. Limited choice in matters of marriage is not the best for any sex, but it's worse for young women who move here single. It's tough I tell you.

Alaba: Naturally.

Kola: Many end up not marrying or making do with whatever they find. You know what I mean.

Alaba: I think so. But I also think there are more than enough choices. You don't have to look for a Nigerian or even a black. There are so many white gals around. That is one of the beauties of a country like this. Interracial unions can be great.

Kola: Coming back to job prospect. From the way you are talking, I believe you will be better off financially and more useful to our country back home with all the trainings and exposure you've had here.

Alaba: You are not entirely wrong. If fact you are right.

Kola: So what are you waiting for?

Alaba: For a better deal.

Kola: I see. Are you sure a better deal will ever come and will that replace your value for our people at home.

Alaba: Not at all, but thank God skill and technology transfer knows no geographical boundary in this internet age. So a lot can still be done even when you are here.

However, in my own case, there is an urgent need to impact my place of birth positively, so it won't be very long from now before you begin to see me mostly in Nigeria.

Kola: Good one. I will wait a little bit for a better deal too and if not begin to look elsewhere or back home. Honestly it makes sense.

Alaba: It does.

I looked at him reassuringly.

Alaba: Be happy my brother. Your future is bright. You are doing your best to ensure that.

Kola: Yes.

Alaba: Anyway, catch you later.

Kola: Bye.

My Job Search Experience

When I got to Calgary for my internship training, I needed to find a place to work so I can pay my bills since internship positions were not paid positions. I was at various job search seminars facilitated by Alberta Works. At a job fair, the first I would attend in Calgary, I got interviewed by a human resources personnel from Sears Canada.

I actually attended the desks of various companies and departmental stores in Calgary like, Bed, Bath, and Beyond, Marks, Safeway, Sport Check etc.

The question you want to ask me is, what has working in these places got to do with my pharmacy training? Am I not supposed to be a skilled migrant? I was a federal skilled worker migrant who was given a permanent resident status from Nigeria based on my skills and experience.

Well, I have no answer to your question because I was as surprised as you might imagine and in fact had moved past the stage of asking these questions.

Thank God, I am on my path to getting licensed in Canada. My day job will be my internship training, but because that is not paid, I have to look for a night job.

On my way back home from the job fair, my phone rang.

Caller: Hello.

Alaba: Hi.

Caller: My name is Sandra Walker (not real name). I am of Sear Canada's Human Resources.

Alaba: "Ooh." I sat up in my seat in the bus.

Caller: Am I speaking with Alaba?

Alaba: Yes. Speaking.

Caller: I interviewed you earlier this afternoon at the job fair.

Alaba: Oh. Yes, I was there.

Caller: I am happy to inform you have been offered the position.

Alaba: That's quick!!! Thank you for that.

Caller: Did you say you prefer to work at night?

Alaba: I wouldn't dictate my schedule to you but you are right. I prefer the night schedule.

Caller: Yes, the night schedule will give you a few dollars more and also a few hours more.

Alaba: Thank you for that.

Caller: When do you wish to start?

Alaba: I can start anytime you want me to.

Caller: Okay. First, you will need to attend employment training. One will be coming up next Monday. (That was a Friday). We will send an electronic version of your offer of employment with some materials you need to go through before your training.

Alaba: Thank you. And thank you very much for the offer.

Caller: You are most welcome. Do you have any questions for me at the moment?

Alaba: Not at all. I will be expecting the email, then will be at the training Monday.

Caller: Bye for now, Alaba.

Alaba: Bye bye, Ms Sandra.

I attended the training. As always in Canada, training was good, and lots of things learnt that will be useful even not on the prospective job.

I like to attend any form of training I am invited because you can never go wrong learning new things or even refreshing old knowledge, skills, and idea. There is always value added.

The following day, I was job ready. But then, my oral structured clinical examination was coming up in 3 weeks. I put a call through to my wife who was still in Toronto with the kids. Her phone rang.

Alaba: Hello dear.

Eniola: Hi darling.

Alaba: How are you guys doing?

Eniola: Fine.

Alaba: Hope the kids are not bugging you too much?

Eniola: What can I do? You know kids now. We are doing very fine.

Alaba: I just got a job now.

Eniola: Great!!! What job is that?

Alaba: The one at Sears.

I wanted to mention the job title, but my lips got stuck. Why? I don't know. It was involuntary. But that was not normal with me. I noted that. A sign my mind was not really at peace with what was happening to me. Just putting up a bold front.

Eniola: You told me "material handler."

Alaba: Yes, material handler, whatever that mean.

Eniola: I am still not clear what that really mean too.

Alaba: From my training, I've come to know it's like people loading, unloading and packaging goods at warehouse.

Eniola: Hmm. The title sounds so fanciful.

Alaba: You can say that again. I guess the title "loader" or 'loading or unloading personnel" has gone out of vogue, so they coined such a fanciful name. The fact is I will be loading and unloading merchandise at night.

Eniola: And who would want to or should I say not want to hire a pharmacist as a loader? That gives higher level of capacity to their work force, so they grabbed you.

Alaba: Hmmmm

Eniola: This is ridiculous!

Alaba: You can say that again, but do I have a choice? I have already boarded this "one chance" taxi.

Eniola: And you think you can do that? You have not done anything like that all your life.

Alaba: Do I have a choice? At this point, any job that can pay a little of my bill will do.

Eniola: Hmm. You have a point.

Alaba: I need the pay, and that's what matters to me right now. In fact, I have started calculating the pay, 13.5 dollars per hour, and 24 hours per week. That comes to almost 1300 dollars per month. That will solve a little of my problems you know.

Eniola: And you will be working at night?

Alaba: Yes, that is my best bet, so I can do my training in the day.

Eniola: I am just concerned. That will give you a lot of stress.

Alaba: But you know I am up to the task.

Eniola: Yes, I know you can but what of your exams? Your exam comes up 3 weeks from now. You have been preparing hard for your exams. That is the primary reason you moved to Calgary, and I don't want us to jeopardize that.

Alaba: I see your point but I need the money. So what do I do?

Eniola: You are not used to staying up late in the night. In fact you sleep right after the news around 9 pm. Now you talk of working overnight, going for your internship and also preparing for your exams. Combining all these will be very hard on you.

Alaba: I get your point, but in this situation what do I do?

Eniola: I suggest you don't go to the work now. Tell them to hold it for you for the next 3 weeks. Then you can start.

Alaba: And you think that will work?

Eniola: It takes a while for someone to adjust his body to night work and the disruptions in sleep cycle that will follow. Think of the adjustment process. You cannot afford to be adjusting to something you are not used to when you are preparing for your exams. That could be disastrous. I don't want your exams jeopardized because of little money.

Alaba: But I don't want to lose the job. And like I told you I already calculated my pay. My mind is fixed on it.

Eniola: Which jobs are we talking about you don't want to lose? The Material Handler, night job? Common. If they take it, you'll find another one.

Alaba: Not as easy as you think. Anyway, I already bought my gloves; steel toed footwear, my touch light and what have you. I also have bought my bus tickets, so no going back.

Eniola: I'll prefer you hold on till after your exams.

Alaba: Okay, I'll think about it.

I told her that just to end the discussion, I had made up my mind to start. God knows this was just for economic reasons. I feared going bankrupt and not having money to spend for my daily needs, and if I did not take urgent steps, that was very imminent. Remember I was in Calgary and my family in Toronto, so we needed to maintain 2 locations.

The following evening, I prepared myself and headed to work. It was about 1-hour travel from my place. I would be taking 2 buses and a train. And work from 10pm to 6am 3 nights a week.

I got there that night, got in the reception and was met by the security at the entrance to the main building. The security guard, a black man most probably Nigerian or at least West African from his accent and nametag called out me:

Security Guard: Hello man.

Alaba: Good evening, I am here to work tonight.

Security Guard: Are you part of the night crew?

Alaba: Yes.

He must have easily noticed I was new because while I was there a number of people punched in some numbers and went in.

Security Guard: Where is your pass?

Alaba: I've not been issued any.

Security Guard: What is your name?

Alaba: Alaba Ojapinwa.

Security Guard: Any I.D.?

Alaba: Yes, here it is.

I handed out my driver's license. He looked through a book and pointed to a name.

Security Guard: Yes, I have your name here. It says you need to submit your signed acceptance of offer.

Alaba: I already did that and faxed it to them yesterday.

Security Guard: Perhaps it was not processed before they left office.

Alaba: What does that matter? If I don't want to take the offer, would I have attended the training? Or would I be here to resume work?

Security Guard: Yes. I understand what you mean, but there is a procedure I have to follow.

Thoughts were racing through my head and mind. I hope this man was not going to stop me from working tonight. I came here in this very cold evening, travelling over one and half hours due to delays!!! Nobody is going to turn me back!!!

I have calculated how much I would make that night in my brain, 108 dollars before tax. Hopefully it won't be taxed since its low wage. This is the first time I would be working in Canada so let's wait till I am paid after 2 weeks, then I will know.

"You know I have to follow procedure," that was the security guard. I was beginning to loathe his stance. How can this man bring up this to block me?

Alaba: Can you put a call through to the team lead? I understand we have a team lead here and he should be expecting me.

Security Guard: Okay if you insist, I will do that to satisfy you.

He moved over to the phone and dialed a number.

Security Guard: Hello Gerald (not real name), I have a gentle man by name Alaba here. He said he is part of your crew.

"Yes I can see his name here but his documents are not complete yet."

"Yes I know we can't let him in. he seems not to believe me so I thought I should call you in his presence to confirm that thanks."

He dropped the phone.

Security Guard: You see? It can't work. Don't you have a car? You can quickly drive down, bring the documents and work tonight.

Alaba: No. I don't drive and I live far from here.

Security Guard: That will be hard then. So endeavor to bring your documents tomorrow, so you can start.

Alaba: Bye.

I turned and left the place. There was no point to continue grandstanding.

In the bus, on my way home, I wasn't happy. I haven't done anything wrong, but I have had a mindset of starting work that night. During the training, I was even assured there was a career progression pathway whereby going forward, I may be "lucky" to be trained as a forklift operator where I may be earning up to 20 dollars per hour, perhaps 3 to 4 years down the road or a supervisor 3 or 4 years down the road where I would be a proud earner of up to 16 to 18 dollars per hour. Lucky me!!

This was now supposed to be the super dream of a federal skilled worker starting off in Canada as a merchandiser loader with the fanciful job title "material handler"! And still unhappy with the prospect of losing that "opportunity"!! What a life!!!

To be sure, I have been a very humble person by all considerations. This is by confessions of people who have taken time to interact with me anyway. But this very experience was so humbling and expository. It still has significant positive impact in my life till this day and to the effect we humans are essentially blind and in the real sense may never have an idea of what may be our lot as we go about pursuing our career and life goals.

The grass seems greener in the other end of the pasture, but it may not really be so. This is one more reason to fear God. He is the only one who knows the end even before the beginning.

I got home at about 1 am in the night. I did not want to call my wife. Did not want to disrupt her sleep. I would call her in the morning. She will be happy if only I would put off this night material handler job until after my exams for obvious reason. That has been her proposal. And I eventually did just that.

After my examination, I went ahead to complete my internship under David Mbong, my senior from University of Benin Nigeria. He later became our instructor and guide in pharmaceutics practical classes in the faculty laboratory. I remember he was a fine gentleman. Fate would bring us together again in Canada. It happened through the instance of Professor M.A Iwuagwu, who happens to be mentor to both of us at different times.

I had gone to visit Professor Iwuagu in his office during the time I was working on my Masters in Public Health degree. He knew I had been in Canada and so asked how far I had gone with my licensure. I told him I was having challenges getting internship position.

Prof. Iwuagwu: Do you know David?

Alaba: Which David?

Prof. Iwuagwu: David Mbong. He was our student here and my friend.

Alaba: I think I know him. He used to demonstrate for us at the pharmaceutics laboratory.

Prof. Iwuagwu: Exactly.

Alaba: He was driving a BMW. He has a fair complexion.

Prof. Iwuagwu: You remember him. He was doing his M.Phil. And working towards a Ph.D.

Alaba: Yes. Is he in Canada?

Prof. Iwuagwu: Yes. I will connect the two of you again. He is a good guy and will be very helpful in making you settle down really fast.

Alaba: I need it sir.

Prof. Iwuagwu: OK. Here is his phone number. Please give him a call when you get back to Canada.

Alaba: Very well sir.

Prof. Iwuagwu: I would have called him beforehand and you carry on from there.

Alaba: Thank you very much Prof. What can I do without you?

Prof. Iwuagwu: You are welcome. What are we here for?

Alaba: Thanks Prof.

So I eventually got across to David who did everything to link me up to places and people in Toronto, so I didn't have to go through the stress of relocating to Calgary, Alberta because of an internship. When all efforts proved futile, he advised me to move to Calgary so that I could do my internship with him. I did just that. And as you would imagine the internship training was smooth and seamless.

I would eventually get licensed and work as relief pharmacist for six months before getting a full time position in one of the pharmacy chains in Canada.

David remains my mentor until today. The relationship between us and our families is more like brother to brother.

While on my internship and after I missed my "material handler" job position with Sears, I threw my application around and eventually landed a job with a security provider company G4S security as a night operator. My responsibilities included:

- Filling shifts with security guards (scheduling)
- Managing book offs by guards
- Taking shift coverage demands from clients

Checking on guards while on shifts, providing information to them, answering their questions, and escalating issues to my superior and colleagues as necessary.

And many other responsibilities.

It was a job that required full alertness, quick judgment and decision-making. The seven months or so that I spent with them was very rewarding and invaluable as far as developing these and many other skills. It was made more interesting, by Roger Agard, the then Western Control Manager with whom my family and I are still in touch with today.

Foreign Credentials and Experience not Generally Recognized.

Foreign credentials and experience are not recognized in Canada, for the most part.

Most often than not, people have to begin again to navigate the path to their professional qualifications. In many cases, there are limited training positions for even for those who qualify, placing them as warehousing professionals for years and stagnating them. This situation has the potential to have significant negative implications on ever having the opportunity to practice ever again. The reason is that, in many cases, you can only be out of your profession for so many years to be considered still current and trainable. Some never get training positions even though qualified while some don't qualify eventually. This has disastrous social, psychological and financial consequences.

Most skilled workers spend the first two to three years and money trying to get qualified here. And only the fortunate and or lucky ones make it in this time span since it commonly takes much longer.

The major barrier to getting a job in Canada, especially in the urban areas where migrants tend to congregate, is the issue of lack of "Canadian Experience". The lowest job positions, even volunteer positions, require Canadian experience for most employers. In other words, employers were not inclined to invest in a lot of time in training new people. And who would blame them? It is just the natural law of demand and supply at play. There are simply too many people for the available positions.

People have described "Canadian experience" requirements as a ploy by employers to systematically screen out skilled migrant workers from suitable jobs due to the limited labor market.

This is not unexpected, since Canada has decided to put the cart before the horse. Instead of ascertaining its labor needs and identifying job prospects to a reasonable degree before bringing skilled workers in, they do it the other way around. They also either knowingly or unknowingly bring in too many skilled migrants in the same field, only for professional bodies and employers to discount their experience and education. This sets them up for the likelihood of not getting into their expected roles. Many people have been set up to fail from the start.

It is very difficult to excuse the government of Canada from complicity in this matter.

The truth is, some of the world's best and brightest sometimes struggle to find work in Canada.[6] Visiting Canada briefly on vacation and spending your money to view and experience the beautiful landscape, sceneries, cities, historical and other tourist attractions is far different from settling down economically. Many skilled professionals are on record of having lost significant savings trying to fit in after coming here with their funds. They have had to leave after many unsuccessful attempts at finding an appropriate job. It is not that they are too picky or particular about jobs, but most times, what you get is not even close to your education, experience or former income.

Most skilled workers who moved to Canada are university graduates. Yet these immigrants are mostly unemployed or underemployed.

According to some sources, more than half of immigrants to Canada in recent years have come in as skilled workers.

When it comes to matching skills and education to jobs, Canada is one the worst countries in the world. This is because there are just too many qualified individuals.

---

[6] Tamsin MacMahon; April 2013. Macleans. Global Issues. Our Insights, Why the World's Best and Brightest Struggle to Find Jobs in Canada. Why do Skilled Immigrants Often Fare Worse Here Than in The US and UK? (accessed March 10,2016). macleans.ca.

The unemployment and underemployment of immigrants definitely presents huge cost to the economy. The loss in opportunity and productivity can be huge especially in a country like Canada where social insurance for the unemployed is still taken very seriously. The career, financial and social stagnation, decline and loss of many skilled immigrants are incalculable and many destinies have been changed forever.

The Organization for Economic Cooperation and Development (OECD) estimated the number of Canadian immigrants living in poverty to be 23 percent compared to the global average of 17 percent.[7]

According to past OECD statistics, only about 60 percent of Canadian skilled migrants were working in jobs requiring skilled workers. This does not mean that this 60 percent are working in their field compared to global OECD average of 71 percent. The statistics may even be worse now.

Because of the huge influx of skilled migrant workers, which is much more than what Canada actually needs, a buyer's market has been created where the employers are now calling the shots. With the abundant pool of skilled workers, they invented the Canadian Experience mantra. It means that you only stand a very small chance of being employed if you don't have Canadian experience. You cannot get entry-level jobs or even a grocery clerk or attendant job in some extreme cases if you don't have Canadian experience.

How does a new skilled migrant get Canadian experience? Is it inside the aircraft while coming from Asia, Europe, Africa or wherever? This way, immigrants hardly get a chance to put a foot in the door. Many are therefore stagnated. Many view this as discriminatory against skilled migrants, which is true.

---

[7] Organisation for Economic Cooperation and Development. OECD: Better Policies for Better Lives. Indicators of Integration 2012. Key Indicators by Country: Canada. Canada-OECD (accessed March 12, 2106) https://www.oecd.org/immigration/integration-indicators-2002.

Personally, I see the Canadian Experience requirements of a federal skilled migrant as foolish pride on the part of the prospective Canadian employer. You would think that a smart employer would look deeper into what different perspectives, views, approaches and skills a foreign trained would bring to bear to tasks assigned him due to his different background. Some of these can be tapped. Who knows? Instead, they tend to ignore the benefits international experience and perspectives can have on society by using Canadian experience as a weeding tool. This missed opportunity is monumental. Again, it is a situation of demand and supply.

This situation has resulted in the creation of a booming job search coaching, volunteering, and employment agency industry. Instead of the authority to quickly respond and acknowledge the problem that they have created in the skilled labor market, they have acted like an ostrich by creating many job searching centers.

This is an attempt to put the blame on the migrant. The narrative was that their job search skills were not sharp enough, so they needed help. This has done little other than further create jobs for the experienced citizens. The success that can be attributed to this approach is that it keeps skilled migrants in front of computers and in job search seminars which are widely available in the cities.

Tell me who needs job search trainings and professional job search middlemen if the jobs are really out there.

By their own inadvertent confession, you hear the job search trainers in training and workshops say that most jobs are hidden. We, therefore, get training on how to explore the hidden job market. How would a new immigrant with little or no social ties find a job that some people have decided to hide because they are afraid that migrants might get the job on a level playing field?

That was a systemic exclusionist strategy.

Many migrants have unpleasant stories to tell about this. In Ontario, I looked for volunteer opportunities for over one year without success. I then relocated to Calgary, Alberta, which was a flight of almost four hours before I could find a place to have my first training and work experience in Canada. This was with my Nigerian Connection.

Of course, you would not expect an employer to just bring in a foreign trained migrant based on Immigration Canada screening, but not getting even a chance for an interview is because employers are inundated with resumes and, therefore, the natural law of demand and supply kicks in.

We must not take our focus off the fact that Immigration Canada is the gate keeper that created this abnormal situation which has adversely impacted the future of many brilliant men and women and their families.

Many skilled migrants have sold their properties and resigned jobs in their home countries in order to migrate to Canada. As a result, returning to their home countries is not possible.

What I advocate for anyone leaving his home country is to have a plan B (an exit strategy). Therefore, if things don't work out, you have a plan to come back to your comfort zone to become productive again. It is called reverse migration and there is nothing wrong with that.

Many have been forced to remain here for the sake of family and survival. It is an irony that somebody who migrated to better the situation of himself, his family and future generations, now finds himself worse off.

Many resort to the mantra "we are here because of our children". However, the kind of work that they do and the time spent at work just to make ends meet does not leave much time to pay attention to their children. This situation does not bring out the best in these children and may actually bring out the worse. This is because, for the most part, they are left to the vagaries of negative societal and peer influence. This is because their parents who are supposed to be around to guide them by spending quality time with them cannot afford to.

Migration the Bad

Most people who claim to be here because of kids will have only 1 or 2 children. What an irony!!! I am not advocating that people have more children against their wishes and plans, but if you claim to be here because of something, then you had better have enough of that thing. Pardon my "warped' opinion.

But how would a young couple have more children or even young men and women plan to get married and have families when daycare costs so much? Most of the young families prefer to let one of the parents work while other cares for the children or one works nights while the other works during the day until the kids are old enough to stay home alone. This is one of the recipes for disastrous and broken homes.

However, there are still prospects in the trade industry such as construction, welding, forklift operators, trucking etc., if you can quickly attend college in order to get a diploma. This will allow you to find job easier than going to the university to obtain multiple degrees with which you might not find jobs but will get into debt. Going to the university here does not guarantee anyone job placement. There are many Ph.D. holders who are driving taxis. Therefore, getting a Canadian education does not necessarily translate into getting a Canadian job in that field.

One of my friends frankly said he would prepare his graduate son's mind to go in forklift driving or similar training, as soon as he arrived from Nigeria so he could hit the ground running in the economy.

How can you expect job opportunities and job mobility from a country with a small population and a high knowledge and skill level? Canada has one of the highest numbers of educated and skilled workers per capita in the world. Many Canadians have had to leave Canada for greener pastures, since the job situation in Canada has been getting worse.

Part of the problem is outsourcing. Many Canadian businesses like in most of the west, outsource many of their production and services overseas in order to be globally competitive, thereby reducing the hope of better job prospects for its residents. The result is that job prospects, opportunities, career growth, etc. may be better in the emerging markets of Asia and Africa when corrected for the same level of knowledge, skill, and training.

The lesson to be learned is once you are established professionally and financially in your home country, you have to think twice before moving to the western world. There must be compelling reasons or extenuating circumstances to leave that relative certainty for uncertainty.

I have a personal story to tell about foreign credential recognition in Canada. Let's start with the English language requirements. English is the official language in Nigeria. Since it is a former colony of Britain, and a multi-language multi-ethnic country, it is natural the language of instruction in school from the lowest to highest levels of education is the English language.

It is difficult to adopt any of the numerous languages as official. Attempts have been made to design or evolve a language from the three main languages of Hausa, Igbo and Yoruba in what the proponents christened WAZOBIA coined from wa, zo and bia which in English translates to COME in the three major languages WA- Yoruba, ZO- Hausa and BIA- Igbo. These attempts have not been successful and have not been given serious consideration.

The languages are spoken at home, but officially, the English language is everywhere. As matter of fact, for many Nigerians in cosmopolitan areas like, Lagos, Abuja, Port Harcourt, Kaduna, Kano, Enugu etc., and in many families, English language is the first language and the language spoken at home. There are many families that are getting criticism for that.

Many of these Nigerians come to Canada and often bewildered that they cannot claim English language to be their first language. Meanwhile, many of them do not even understand any other language save the english language. Double jeopardy! What an irony!!

By the time I got to Toronto, I had used English language actively for at least 30 years. My education from grade 1 to second degree was in the English language. My professional practice and communication for 11 years before that was also in the English language. I have written articles in the national newspaper and I have published a book in the English language. On top of everything, I have written the International English Language Test IELTS, administered by the British Council and which is the standard test for English proficiency three times and have passed brilliantly every time. I have written the academic version twice and the General Training version once.

I, therefore, had no doubt in my mind that I was proficient enough to communicate in English.

I got to Toronto, and in my effort to get integrated into my new country as quickly as possible, I got my documents evaluated and applied for the evaluating examination which would be seven months after I got into the country. There was considerable study and preparation to be done. I attempted to get a pharmacy assistant or clerk job while preparing for my evaluating exams. I tried hard but couldn't secure a position. My main obstacle was a lack of Canadian experience. You might wonder how a new immigrant would have Canadian experience. If he were not given a chance of getting a foot in the door, how would he ever get started? I tried many pharmacies and a couple of hospitals. Then I shrugged my shoulders and said that was fair, perhaps after my evaluating examinations, I would have a chance.

I passed the examination. The next step is to enroll for the qualifying examination. If you are very brilliant and worked hard you could pass the written part of the qualifying examination at once but most people need to have practical experience in a pharmacy to have a good chance of passing the second part which is the OSCE Oral Structural Clinical Examination. It is a live examination where the practice situation is simulated in different scenarios. Different actors and materials and situations are presented to the candidates in a stipple chase mode. To me it is a very good way of judging clinical judgment, interaction, communication skill, therapeutic knowledge and many other competencies.

I had figured that having practical experience would come in handy. In fact, it was necessary before going for such exam.

Therefore, I picked up my credentials, my evaluation exam results and other necessary things and started going from pharmacy to pharmacy looking for a spot to volunteer so I could get the hands-on experience that I really needed.

I went to so many pharmacies and met many proprietors. Some of them you have to go to several times before getting a chance to meet them. Sometimes you may see them but they do not have the time to talk to you.

When you eventually meet them, the usual response from is usually one or more of the following;

"We don't need anybody now."

"Have you had Canadian experience in pharmacy practice?"

Are you licensed in Canada? Etc.

Why ask a new migrant if he has Canadian experience? It is hypocrisy!

I had the following exchange with one of them.

Alaba: Hello sir, good afternoon. My name is Alaba. I am a foreign trained pharmacist from Nigeria.

Proprietor: You are welcome. I am Jake (not real name).

Alaba: Nice meeting you today Mr. Jake. Actually, I've been here a couple of times to try to see you.

Proprietor: Ooh. What can I do for you?

Alaba: I am a permanent resident who just passed the Pharmacy Examining Board of Canada (PEBC) evaluating examination.

Proprietor: Congratulations.

Alaba: Thank you sir. The next step for me is the qualifying examination, but I need a good deal of preparation before that.

Proprietor: That's right. It's good to prepare well.

Alaba: Yes. And one of the key components is to have hands-on experience.

Proprietor: That's right.

Alaba: I have tried to see you couple of times to no avail. I would like to volunteer in your pharmacy for 3 to 6 months. This is my resume for your review, sir.

He looked away for a moment and turned back to me.

Proprietor: Young man, there are a couple of issues here.

Alaba: Yes, sir.

Proprietor: For one, we do not have a space for an extra person, so we cannot accommodate you for now.

Two, for you to be a student, there are some requirements. Have you been to the Ontario College of Pharmacists?

Alaba: No, but I have gone through their website and I have a good idea of their requirements and licensure processes.

Proprietor: Anyway, I will advise you go there physically with your credentials or at least give them a call. (He provided a phone number) This is their phone number.

Alaba: OK, sir. I will do so. But can I drop my resume with you so whatever happen and when there is a space, I can be considered?

Proprietor: No. I am sure there will not be a spot in the near future, so there is no need to take the resume.

Alaba: Thank you.

I had more than 50 of these encounters within a 6 week period. The more charitable proprietor will take the resume from me, but you will never hear from him or her again. I made follow-up phone calls and repeat visits to some of them, which in my own eyes would possibly be considered a futile waste of time.

I was familiar with the Ontario College of Pharmacists procedures and requirements. As of 2011, a foreign trained pharmacist had to attend a bridging program at the University of Toronto. The program was intended to "brush up" international graduates to Canadian standards, so the qualifying exams and fitting into the practice environment would be seamless. It was called the international pharmacy graduates (IPG) bridging program. It was a two-semester program. It was a very intensive two semesters of three months each, totaling 6 months. It was expensive too, at least for me. It cost about 14,000 dollars, although as usual, loans were available for those who needed them. Most international graduates needed the loan. The program was a product of research into how to best integrate international graduates into the Canadian practice environment or at least the Ontario practice environment.

A couple of days after my encounter with the proprietor, I prepared myself and went to the University of Toronto. I was ready for the program even though I was convinced that I could pass the examinations otherwise. I was sure that I would pass the written part of the exam as long as I had the materials, a library around me and the time to study.

Therefore, I went to the office of the coordinator of the program at the University of Toronto, knocked on the door and went in. The following dialogue ensued:

Alaba: Good morning.

Coordinator: Good morning, how can I help you today?

Alaba: My name is Alaba. I am an international pharmacy graduate. I would like to enroll for the next IPG (International Pharmacy Graduate) program.

Coordinator: Ok. That's good.

Alaba: I have my credentials here for you to check.

Coordinator: Mr. Alaba. The procedure is for you to submit those at the office. When it gets to my table, I will review them and we will communicate with you.

Alaba: I very much understand that and have a copy of each with your secretary.

Coordinator: Ok.

Alaba: Since I am lucky to meet you this morning, I would appreciate if you quickly go through my documents so I will know if anything has been left out.

Coordinator: OK. I'll do that quickly. (She collected the documents from me and looked through each of them).

She then picked out one of the documents and looked at me.

Alaba: I looked at her. I did not envisage any problems since I had gone through all of the requirements and check listed all of them before heading there.

Oh, I thought. Did I mix up any of my documents?

Coordinator: I am afraid there is a problem with this.

She handed me my IELTS (International English Language Testing System) results sheet.

Alaba: What is the problem with it?

Coordinator: It is not current.

Alaba: How?

Coordinator: You see the next program starts in September. This result expires August 31.

Alaba: Uhmm.

As part of the qualifications for permanent residence, I have had to submit an evidence of my proficiency in the English language to the Canadian High Commission Ghana. I wrote both the Academic and General versions. The IPG (International Pharmacy Graduate) program required the academic version. That was my third time of writing and passing the test. I had written it for different purposes.

The result expires every two years. It's very funny that they think that the English proficiency of a more or less native speaker would not be current after two years. We generally believed that was unfair.

However, I had gone to the coordinator with the impression that all my credentials were current as of that date.

Alaba: So what do I do now?

Coordinator: You will have to provide a current English Proficiency Proof, since every credential has to be current at the inception of the program.

Alaba: But this is still current.

Coordinator: But by the time the program starts, it would have expired by a couple of days.

Alaba: But by my English skills would not have expired. I can assure you I will still be able to use the English language properly and that would not be a problem for anybody. So if the essence of this is to ensure poor English language skills do not come between my learning and integration, then there is no problem.

The coordinator was looking at me, waiting for me to finish my unsolicited "speech".

Coordinator: Anyway, that is the way it is.

Alaba: If at any point in the program, you find that the English language becomes an issue, I will sign an understanding then you can remove me from the program.

Coordinator: Hmmm

Alaba: It seems to me this is just been employed as a screening tool to take some people out of the program due to oversubscription.

Coordinator: Uhmm.

Alaba: I would appreciate it if you would let me register now. I will then go ahead to register for the English test. Between registration, writing the test and getting the results may take up to three weeks. Sure I will pass it. I have written it three times and I always passed. This way I would be able to start the program.

Coordinator: No. It does not work that way. Like I said, everything has to be current from inception.

Alaba: So what do I do now?

Coordinator: Wait for the next session.

Alaba: Next session?

Coordinator: Yes. And I have to advise you to get your documents in early since we receive very many applications.

Alaba: So what should I be doing for the next 8-9 months?

Coordinator: Try to find a job to do to kill the time.

Alaba: I have tried to apply for some jobs, but I have had no favorable responses even for pharmacy assistant or clerk positions. This is not to mention pharmacy technician positions.

Coordinator: It does not necessarily have to be in the pharmaceutical industry or even the health sector. You may try to find positions in other areas. That was what I had to do, when I got here as an immigrant years ago. That is what most foreign trained professionals do.

Alaba: You mean to try applying for a security job, a factory worker, or a trailer loader?

Uhmm. I see what you mean.

I could see impatience growing in her.

Alaba: Anyway, I assure you I will prepare privately for these examinations and pass them. This is what I said as I closed the door behind me.

I did pass. But not without some time and effort expended.

That again brought up the issue of oversupply of skilled migrants. Would anybody tell me that the IPG (International Pharmacy Graduate) program would invoke the English language expiration mantra if the program were undersubscribed? That was the beginning of my travail in getting licensed in Canada.

My first reaction after this encounter was to prepare to leave Canada and go back to Nigeria to work so I could sustain my family from there until my next examination. I saw no sense in becoming a factory worker who would work and get so tired that I wouldn't even be able to study and prepare for the examinations. I felt that I would be more productive and successful with the integration if I left Canada for a while. What a paradoxical way of thinking. But that would have been the better option for me. The plan was to buy all of the necessary texts and materials. I did buy many materials for Canada and United States examinations.

In Nigeria, I would make more money doing my professional job, and would still have sufficient time and space to study for my examinations. I only hoped that I would still have the opportunity in the future to have a couple of months of practical experience in a community outlet in Canada. This would help to familiarize myself with the nuances of the practice at least in that setting so I am better prepared for the oral structured clinical examination. But that plan was not to be!

In addition, my wife was heavy and due in September.

Oooh: I had been deep in thought.

OK. I would wait for my wife to be put to bed, stay with her for a little while so she could become fit and able to support herself and the children in the domestic chores, clinic visits, school runs and their general care. Then I could quickly go back, make some money, and study hard so that my qualification will be quicker and smoother. Then when the child got to daycare age, my wife could start her own career plan, since hopefully by then, I would have gotten my license.

Definitely, I must still be in dreamland. My wife put to bed in September, and three months later, it became crystal clear to me there was no way I could leave her alone to take care of all necessary family runs with the newborn and other 2 kids. If I left, there was no other support. Staying was the only reasonable thing to do. Reality had dawned on me. We were no longer in Nigeria where you have the support of family, friends, and neighbor's support. This was Canada. You are on your own, as far as these domestic runs and childcare are concerned. It was a clear reality check.

Therefore, I settled in to continue my job search, attend employment training, job fairs, and sessions with job search and employment consultants. Of course, I continued to prepare for my next examinations. I must confess those searches and training had a very significant impact on my personal and character development. Here I was , a professional who had practiced for over 10 years, owned a practice, and was running a good and progressive life going to job fairs, and applying for below the line jobs in a new and completely strange environment. I had no success with the job search and with no sign of success. With all these activities, I still needed to prepare and qualify to practice here. There were no guarantees and many factors were outside of my control. The stakes were really very high. It was very humbling and a very difficult test of character.

It was a very rude awakening. I definitely came out of the situation a way better person in all respects.

After months of waiting and having prepared through private studies and attending preparatory classes, I gave practical experience another thought. I again started going around to pharmacies with my resume in the hope of getting a spot in a volunteer position as a pharmacy assistant or clerk so I could have a good shot at the qualifying examination. Again, it was no go. To be a student, as you would be called in that situation, you have to be in the University of Toronto's IPG (International Pharmacy Graduate) bridging program.

However, I had an encounter with an elderly pharmacist that gave me a ray of hope. The hope never came to reality. This is how the encounter went in this very spacious pharmacy.

Alaba: Hello sir.

Pharmacist: Hello, young man.

Alaba: My name is Alaba, an international pharmacy graduate from Nigeria. I am looking for a volunteer position in your pharmacy.

Pharmacist: I see. When did you arrive in Canada?

Alaba: One year ago.

Pharmacist: Have you ever worked in Canada?

Alaba: No. I have had to prepare for evaluating examinations, which I passed and then went on to preparing for the qualifying examination.

Pharmacist: I see. So, how far did you get with that?

Alaba: I have prepared extensively for that. I have 10 years of continuous practice as a pharmacist in Nigeria, so I am still current.

Pharmacist: OK.

Alaba: However, I want to work as a volunteer in your pharmacy so I become more knowledgeable about the nuances of the practice here. I believe that this will help me in my examinations and in my future practice in the long run.

I must also add that I have also been trying to get a job but I am still searching.

Pharmacist: Anyway, you are welcome to Canada, Alaba.

Alaba: Thank you.

Pharmacist: Let me have your resume. Come back on Sunday, anytime from 1pm-5pm. Work will be light then, and then we can talk more about this.

I went there. Of course, I was very prompt and neatly groomed.

Pharmacist: Hi Alaba.

Alaba: Hello, Sir.

Pharmacist: You are just right on time. That is a good sign. I have a feeling you will fit very well into the system.

Alaba: Thank you sir.

After a series of questions and answers back and forth, we a scheduled meeting for another time. He said he would call me.

In the meantime, I did not put all of my eggs in one basket and was trying other places.

Then one day, I called him and went to the store. It was more than 6 weeks after our initial contact.

Alaba: Good afternoon, sir.

Pharmacist: Good afternoon.

Alaba: I am the pharmacist looking for a volunteer position.

Pharmacist: Yes, I remember you.

Alaba: I thought that I should check if I will be able to start anytime soon.

Pharmacist: Why not let's do it this way. Get me a police report, and a medical report.

Alaba: OK.

Pharmacist: The police report, of course you know, is for us to know that you have a clean criminal record, and the medical report to show you are free from communicable diseases.

I cringed! So, I am going to get screened legally and medically for this volunteer position. Not much of a proposal anyway, I thought. Just the way he said it was off-putting.

Alaba: Sir, I am only looking for a volunteer position.

I stated that again for emphasis.

Pharmacist: Yes, of course. I know. Young man, so many people are looking for same position, so you know.

Alaba: That's okay by me. I will get those reports done and send them to you.

Pharmacist: That's a good place to start.

Alaba: I need your contact and mailing details because they would want to send it to you directly. Your business card would do.

Pharmacist: OK. Come in three days from now. I will give them to you then.

Why not now? I thought. Why should I have to come another time to get your contact and mailing details? I wondered.

Alaba: OK.

Pharmacist: Whenever you are talking to anybody, look at the person straight in the eyes. I notice that you tend to look away from me when we talk.

Alaba: Uhmmm. That may be true. But you know it's out of deference to you and has nothing to do with whether I am shy or not telling the truth. I can look anybody in the eye.

Pharmacist: I am aware of that. I see that your engagement is good but needs a little bit of tuning up.

Alaba: Yes, it's cultural. In Africa, like you just said you know, we don't look at an elderly person straight in the eye. It connotes disrespect in our culture, but here, not looking straight in the eyes of whoever you are talking to indicates that you are probably are not telling the truth.

Pharmacist: So, you know all that.

Alaba: Of course, I do. I am working on it. It takes a little while, to adjust to such major cultural differences, especially when talking to an elderly black Canadian person like you. I am sure that a white man wouldn't notice, because I would switch to the culture here.

Pharmacist: I see.

Alaba: That's one of the reasons it's instructive to get a position, so I can get more used to the culture here.

Pharmacist: I see your point.

On the day and time we agreed on, I went there promptly.

Pharmacist: Hi, Alaba.

Alaba: Good Afternoon sir.

Pharmacist: Do you drive?

Alaba: No.

Pharmacist: I have a suggestion for you.

Alaba: Okay.

Pharmacist: I would like to suggest you try out another pharmacy, but the pharmacy is in Scarborough and you may find it more convenient if you drive.

I have no problem going anywhere to get the training I needed. But I just could not help wondering why the sudden change after such a long time of back and forth?

I tried to hide my bewilderment but I guess he noticed.

Pharmacist: He is one of us. He is a Nigerian.

Alaba: Okay, sir.

Realizing that was his own euphemistic way of saying no position, I started to leave.

Alaba: Okay. Thank you. I'll get back to you sir. Thanks.

So, I left and made up my mind never to look for a volunteer position for the purpose of the exam anymore.

I also tried a number of public hospitals and only one of them gave me the hope of getting a volunteer position in the cleaning section and that is if I applied on time, since they receive so many applications. A wonder!

However, I continued looking for a paid job as well as preparing privately for my examinations.

I sat for the examinations and passed the written part but failed the clinical part. This confirms that the knowledge is okay, but the delivery of the knowledge and the patient interaction skills were not up to standard. This was not surprising. I saw it coming.

I would later move to Alberta, Canada to do my internship training at the pharmacy of my senior at the University, David Mbong. With the exposure at David's Bridle Wood Pharmacy in Calgary Alberta, I was able to pass the clinical examination. It is a shame that I had to relocate myself and my family to a province almost a four hour flight away from Toronto in order to get an internship and with a school senior from Nigeria.

It is difficult to imagine the cost in terms of finances in what seems like a second round of migration.

As a matter of fact in recent years, many if not most of the newly licensed pharmacists practicing in Ontario moved out to get licensed in another province, solely for that, and then moved back to turn in their licenses to practice.

The question you want to ask is, if they can go to another province with a supposedly easier pathway to get licensed and then come back to Ontario, why not allow them get licensed in Ontario in the first place. It is another hypocrisy!

I have medical doctor friends from all over who have passed their equivalent examinations, but there has been no space for advanced training. Many of these individuals have been specialists in their countries of origin. Canada only recognizes the medical qualifications of certain countries, which is natural, since they cannot afford to bring in all sorts of doctors from everywhere. You are expected to retrain to fit into the practice here, but there are only so many training spots, which Canadian trained, Canadians who trained overseas, and foreign trained compete for, probably in that order.

The result is a backlog of foreign trained doctors waiting for training positions. You can only wait for so long, because after a number of years of not getting a spot, your practice experience and clinical skills are determined to no longer be current. You will need to renew it and make it current before you can move on. How do you renew it, if you cannot practice? You have to go elsewhere. You probably think and I agree with you that this is fair. How can you say that a doctor who has not practiced in a number of years and is probably working as a security guard, personal support worker or cab driver is still current? As a result, many doctors and other medical professionals that are needed back in their home countries are stagnated and wasting away. This is because they did not see the full picture and were not well informed or led into a false sense of hope when they took the decision to migrate as a skilled professional. And there are thousands of them scattered all over.

Some of them even came together to threaten legal action against them the College of Physicians and Surgeons, which is their regulatory body, for the lack of career progress and stagnation. This included the lucky ones who secured supportive roles like physician assistants etc. in the various hospitals.

A friend moved to Australia to advance his career and stayed put. Many go south of the border to the United States of America to find a place for themselves and, of course, most stayed there. I have a friend who had to leave his family after waiting for many years. He had to go to South Africa to train for about five years, so he could come back to Canada to practice. These are the sacrifices that people have to make after deciding to migrate to Canada as skilled foreign trained professionals. And believe me, it can be tough and life changing.

It is the same for most of the various professionals. High, flying professionals migrate to Canada to become low flying. That is if they would even be able to fly at all. Most are ready to take up low-level positions in their field, but these are not even available most of the time. Therefore, they eat their humble pie and fit themselves anywhere.

In my opinion, if skilled migration does not lead to status elevation and economic development for the skilled migrant, it should not make him worse off. Many of them come out worse off and end up in unskilled jobs. This is the worst nightmare for skilled migrants.

In this situation, all of the major players and stakeholders are the losers: Canada, the source country and the migrant professionals whose career is wasted. This has to stop.

Many skilled couples have migrated to Canada. In the course of trying to get established here, one of them could not make it for one reason or another. This results in tension, disunity and rancor in the family. In those instances, where the wives were the fortunate ones, not many can keep the union together for very long. Complex issues start to develop; such as mutual suspicions, complaints of disrespect, inferiority complexes, deflated egos etc.

These are couples that were very happy together before migrating, but whose happiness in matrimony has been punctuated by the dictates of professional licensure in a foreign country. In some cases, one of them accepts the undesirable and adjusts to the situation. In other cases, adjustments and compromises become difficult and lead to instability and sometimes, eventual decimation of the union.

Couples should be very conscious of these possibilities and make deliberate efforts not to lose their heads when the undesirable events happen as far as the professional recognition, licensure, or advancement of either or two of them are concerned. It should not cause negative attitude. If these attitudes raise their heads, you should make an effort to quickly recognize them and to stop them from festering.

The lesson to be learned here is, once you are established professionally and financially in your home country, it's not worthwhile moving to the western world and leaving certainty for uncertainty unless there are very extenuating circumstances. There have to be compelling personal reasons so that you will be able to cope if things don't go well.

Difficulty in Profitably Running Small Family Businesses

I have met prospective migrants who have the impression they would start a small scale or family business venture when they come to Canada. I believe that the motivation for this line of thought is the entrepreneurial or investor spirit of the economic class that is migrating to Canada. Some of them believe they can just move here and start a restaurant or fast food outlet, grocery store, communication company, pharmacy, confectionery, bakery, farm, transport business, etc. and break even like you can easily do in developing economies.

The question I usually ask them is whether they understand what is meant by a mature economy. The stage of economic development determines the kind of business venture you can start on your own. Most of the businesses in developing economies are sole proprietorships, partnerships, and family businesses. In the western world, franchises and very big chain corporations own most of the businesses. This leaves little or no room for entrepreneurs to make in-roads except in rare cases. Due to lack of job opportunities, some skilled migrants have opted for opening small business and grocery stores because they cannot get jobs that they were trained for. It remains to be seen how they could compete with the grocery retail giants and franchises.

That is why it is preposterous for governments of developing countries to be inviting retail giants to take over retail businesses in their countries. Some are even so proud of merely inviting business people to come that they congratulate themselves and advertise this as an achievement.

In the long run, these retail giants take jobs and the means of livelihood from individuals, families, and society. This is because of corporate greed. New start-up businesses cannot thrive because of corporate competitors who are in better shape financially and know how to meet government regulations. Everyone is forced to work for them, one way or the other.

This brings my focus to the entrepreneur and investor migration program. In my opinion, this has not been successful. Investors who are ready to deposit funds in the country for several years were granted permanent resident status, which leads to citizenship. For a long time, millionaires from around the world bought into the idea and relocated their families.

But then what happens? It is very difficult for entrepreneurs and investors to relocate to a new environment and start over again. To think that because someone who is rich through their business activities in one part of the world can simply move somewhere else and replicate his business success is too simplistic a view. It means that all other factors such as demographics, buying culture, consumption patterns, competition, cost of labor and other characteristics of a market and factors of production are considered immaterial.

So what happens? Only a very small percentage of the investors actually stay or even start any business endeavor at all. The pattern was for them to leave their families, wives and kids to remain in a supposedly more conducive environment to live. The person usually goes back to their home country to be economically productive.

It is very hard to leave a comfortable and successful business to start over again in a completely different country. Most of them eventually find out that it is a recipe for business and financial disaster.

There are many examples of people who have experienced financial and professional failure due to the circumstances they have faced in the host country. This is because they did not see or refused to recognize or acknowledge the impending failures. Some people argue that no matter what happens, the host country ultimately benefits because the principal enters with considerable funds and typically buys a home for his or her family. This boosts the mortgage industry. Many come with a family of four, five, or six. Imagine how many dollars they spend each month. This is especially true if you consider that the principal continues to wire funds from the source country to the host country. Most people who remain in the host country are dependents and under aged children, students, or stay at home mothers and wives who are not economically productive. There is a large capital flight from the various source countries to the host countries. This is very significant if you consider that for nearly twenty years Canada was taking in four to five thousand of these investors every year and the average household was consuming close to five thousand dollars monthly!!

In discussing career progression and business growth, I have seen business people pack up their business and move to Canada.

A senior friend is a confectionary maker in Lagos, Nigeria. He is very successful in his business making what we call "Chin-Chin." He applied to Canada as an entrepreneur and was, of course, granted permanent residence with the intention to become citizen.

He came with his family. On arriving in Canada, he acquired a factory site for his business. There was good access to funds in the form of an industrial loan from the bank; there is no problem with power, which is on 24 hours, skilled labor was available as well as any other infrastructure and amenity that you could think of. The coast seemed very clear and everything was set. Why would a business not do well with all these resources and incentives? You are about to find out.

Three years after starting his business in Canada, I caught up with my senior friend in a mall in Calgary.

Alaba: Hi, Mr. Charles (not real name).

Charles: Whom am I seeing? Alaba!

Alaba: Yes!

Charles: Good to see you! Where have you been?

Alaba: I have been studying and training. I got my license and just started practicing about 2 years ago.

Charles: It must have been a task getting your license.

Alaba: Somehow. The knowledge base is there, the zeal and resources are there, but when you have to combine family issues with getting licensed, it can be a little bit challenging.

Charles: I know. You are up to the task.

Alaba: Yes. After all the rigorous training, you are a much better person professionally and even as an individual.

Charles: I get you point. You are right.

Alaba: How has it been with you, family and business?

Charles: Life has been good. Family is fine. The kids are doing well in school, but as for business, all is not well.

Alaba: How?

Charles: Well, like you know, the entire infrastructure, training and support are available but is that all you need to grow a business? Now I know you need more.

Alaba: No. You still need some other things.

Charles: Like what?

Alaba: You need the market.

Charles: Perfect!!! That's why I like you. Where is the market? Let me tell you. The market is a small one.

Alaba: Yes.

Charles: Market access is the second big issue. You see the market is small. Market access is the bigger issue.

Alaba: Tell me more.

Charles: Okay. See, you produce your stuff. Most grocery store that people patronize here are the big chains. They have a well-established chain of suppliers with whom they have very long relationships. The brands they carry have been around for a long time and they too are not resting on their laurels in market research and product development.

Alaba: You are right.

Charles: You will be surprised that even the few available local grocery stores here have their established suppliers.

Alaba: This is a very mature economy that has been around a long time.

Charles: The small population, presence of grocery chains, and all that are recipe for a monopolistic like economy. These are no places for new players, man.

Alaba: I see your point. Why then are they bringing in people who are entrepreneurs?

Charles: How many people do you know who came in as entrepreneurs that are thriving?

Alaba: Good question. I don't know any really. May be I needed to search deeper.

Charles: Don't waste your time brother. I am a perfect example of how the program does not help. In fact, I pay my mortgage from my business in Lagos.

Alaba: That's not good enough.

Charles: Canada might be good in other areas, but in market access for a new entrepreneur, no show. It is unlike Lagos where you have the market and small players can thrive.

Alaba: That is why I wonder when some governments in Nigeria are now bringing in multinational grocery chains. That is a sure way to destroy local enterprises and the middle class. It is an outdated economic technology.

Charles: Most of our economic policies are way behind current global realities.

Alaba: Yes.

Charles: I will be putting up our factory for sale. I mean the factory here. It is not sustainable in any way.

Alaba: You don't have a choice, if it's not working out.

Charles: Anyway the good thing is I've got a lot of training, skills, and what have you while I am here. I am using these to apply back home and it's bringing very good results.

Alaba: That is what you can't take away from Canada. They will build your skills and train you so much you will be performing at the cutting edge of your profession or business. Canada is one of the best in that regard.

Charles: You are right.

Alaba: And for those who take advantage of it, the skill, knowledge, and technology transfer is one of the reasons that it's still very worthwhile to be in this part of the world.

Charles: Yes, get the skills, training and personnel development. If you ever go back home, you will change and impact many lives positively.

Alaba: Yes.

Charles: Anyway. Great bumping into you today and seeing you are doing okay. I have to go now. Greet your family.

Alaba: Good to chat with you too. Greet your family. Bye.

Charles: Bye.

Huge Household Debts/Non-Remittance

For many migrants, there is a major non-alignment between income and financial commitments. Most migrants are deeply in debt. Household debt is at a record high. This is a gold mine for business owners because it gives them the opportunity to demand more from their employees and to pay them less. If you are not happy, then you can leave. There are many others who are waiting to take your place.

Once you are shackled in debt and the monthly financial commitments in the form of a mortgage, insurance, rent, utility bills etc., you are forced to take any type of job to make ends meet. Fear, dissatisfaction, disillusionment, anger, frustration, and depression will set in. This has the tendency to hurt personal health, relationships, marriage and the society as a whole.

The skilled migrant has been drawn to the new country by a desire to get a better deal for himself, relatives and future generations. The migrant often has been a good provider wherever he was but perhaps he wanted to do more. It takes an average of three years for the skilled migrant to secure a job comparable to what he was doing in his home country, if he ever will. He is, therefore, in a period of financial stagnation. It takes the average family of four or five up to fifty thousand dollars to get by for one year. This is a total of one hundred and fifty thousand dollars in three years. How many people have those kinds of reserves?

The migrant, therefore, soon finds himself with huge credit card debt, study loan and bank debts that he will spend the next five years trying to pay off. To compound his problems, the expectation in his home country and of his family is that he should be doing better to help people financially than he was doing when he was at home. Would you blame people who have these kinds of expectations? Didn't he move to a new country to better his economic lot? Why then would he be worse off now? How would anyone who is just a third party observer and does not experience it first-hand not find this difficult to understand? The truth is that, even for the few who have a higher disposable income than in their country of origin, the discretionary income which is money left to use at your discretion after paying your living expenses such as utilities, rent, or mortgage, insurance, property tax, food, groceries, daycare e.tc is much less than what he had in his country of origin. There is a huge dis-connect between the expectations and the reality as far as remittances are concerned.

The impression financial stability is more assured in the western world for the skilled migrant is more of a myth than the reality. Whenever you are tempted to think that way, you should think again. You must be sure that you have considered the third variable which is selection bias.

My opinion is that unless it is an emergency or they are fleeing from crises, war, disasters, political persecution etc., skilled migrants who have stable careers and incomes should not migrate if they are motivated by the quest of economic gain or freedom. Migration should be directed at finding a comfort zone for one's make up. It should be done with a good knowledge of the values and culture of the country and environment where you are going. There should also be a full assessment of one's own personality and circumstances to see if these fit or connect.

For example, if you have a socialist point of view and believe in "live and let live" and supporting your neighbor in terms of welfare and social fairness, then Canada might be the right place for you. The society has a good social services that can keep you happy since most people around you will be able to afford basic needs of life. This makes everybody happy and enhances the happiness indices of a society. There is also an excellent environment for individuals to thrive. However, if you have a capitalistic bent and all you care about is increasing your material and financial resources, then Canada might not be the right place for you. You may need to search further or be utterly disappointed. When discussing financial freedom and security, while it true that many people fare better when they get to the western world, it is also true that they may fare worse. Doing better financially as an individual and as a family is not automatic. There are many variables and it is very difficult to say what will happen. Things can turn out very poorly if certain measures are not taken and things are not done the way they should be done. It is very easy to go down financially in this part of the world. This is especially true with something like health care costs. You don't want to come here or bring someone here without health care coverage. It could easily result in financial ruin.

My family had gone to visit one of our folks.

Alaba: Aunty, we are here. I called out, after we got into their house. A young man who we later realized was Auntie's son had opened the door for us after we pressed the doorbell.

Aunty: Eheee Alaba, and family! Good to see you guys. She shouted out enthusiastically.

Alaba: Good to see you too Aunty.

It was a Sunday, so everyone was home. Auntie's mother, an octogenarian, also was home. She had been visiting and had been in Canada for about one year. Aunty thought that it had been very wonderful having her around.

"You know the feeling when you have your mother around you. It helps take care of nostalgia to a large extent".

Alaba: I know, it is a wonderful feeling.

Aunty: My siblings in Nigeria and other parts of the world have been fuming about that. They literally have accused me of appropriating our mother to myself.

Alaba: Ha ha ha! It seems so aunty!

Aunty: Let me be, Alaba. Let me enjoy her presence here while it lasts.

Alaba: Hello Mama! I shouted out to Auntie's mother.

Mama: Hi, my son. It is good to see you guys. I noticed a plaster of Paris cast on one of mama's feet. Pointing to the plaster of Paris cast and turning to Aunty.

"Did mama fracture or sprain her foot?" I asked.

Aunty: Yes. It's a long story. I'll tell you. First, let me take care of your beautiful family.

Aunty and Mama quickly went about getting food, drinks and everything for us. They set the dining table for us. This is very typical of African hospitality. Mama was very interesting and graceful. Even at her age, she displayed a high level of agility and intelligence.

Mama: Guys, come over to the table and take good care of yourselves.

We moved over and settled down to devour the sumptuous meal in front of us.

Done with the meal and filled to the brim, I started to ask about Mama's fracture.

Alaba: So Aunty how did it happen? The fracture?

Aunty: En heen! I was going to tell you. Mama has been here for more one year now. As you know, you have to take care of everybody's health coverage. So mama had been covered all long.

A few months ago, I just felt that mama is very healthy and didn't have any health issues. So, I decided not to pay her insurance premium.

Alaba: Why?

Aunty: That was not a good decision. Because barely two months after I stopped paying, mama slipped on the stairs as she was coming downstairs and broke her foot!

Alaba: What!

Aunty: Yes. We came back from the hospital last week. We spent 10 days at the hospital.

Alaba: That's a lot of money that you had to spend.

Aunty: How did you know?

Alaba: I have heard lots of stories about healthcare expenditures for the non-insured. They are not pleasant stories.

Aunty: We spent about 30 thousand dollars in those 10 days.

Alaba: Oh my God!

Aunty: That is the long and short of the story. I thank God we can afford that and my mother is feeling better. However, I regret my decision to suspend payment of the healthcare insurance premium.

Alaba: A lot of people would not be able to afford that. So what would have happened?

Aunty: In Canada, they will still take care of you, but the bill will go on your record for you to pay going forward. Some are never able to pay.

Alaba: I've heard stories of people whose visitors have had health issues on the arrival lounge on their visits to Canada. Fathers who have had heart attacks and mothers who had gone into diabetic coma etc. and had to be rushed to the emergency room. Some of the bills run into hundreds of thousands of dollars.

Aunty: It happened to my friend. Her mother got sick here without health coverage. The hospital bill was about 200 thousand dollars.

Alaba: What!!!

Aunty: To make matter worse, the mother later died shortly after being discharged.

Alaba: Double tragedy!!!

Aunty: And she had to take the corpse home and also foot most of the burial expenses back in Nigeria.

Alaba: Tell me a quicker way to into poverty.

Aunty: None.

Alaba: I agree with you.

Health coverage for anybody coming to this part of the world is a non-negotiable necessity. It is good to get coverage right from the airplane. Anything short of that may turn out to being penny-wise and pound-foolish, and may spell financial doom for the individuals involved.

Loss of Family, Social Ties, and Cultural Identity.

Migration involves moving away from your previous location. The hardest part, however, is being away from your social structure, family, career and everything that had become part of your life. Thank God for the Internet and telephone call capabilities, which have gone a long way to make the world a global village.

Most first generation migrants are not able to get over nostalgic feelings and the loss of career, family and social ties. Internet, social media interactions and phone calls have significantly reduced nostalgia and distance, but it is still a prominent factor. In order to overcome this, many migrants sponsor parents and family members to come and live with them to cushion this effect. This is because annual vacation is not usually more than 2 to 3 weeks and may not be long enough to travel to their home country. If you have kids, it might be too much of a burden physically and financially either to keep them at home when you travel or to take them with you. This is because of the individualistic structure of the society and the relative absence of extended family relationships.

The narrative of subsequent generations or a child who migrated as a child or teenager is different though. While the skilled migrant or parent would still be attached to his country of origin and reflect on a lost career, and social, economic, cultural, religion, family connections and other things, the children have not really experienced this. It is especially true because they were very young when their parents moved or were born in the new adopted country. They would not have experienced any real loss of any of these things and, therefore, see the experience in a different light and may never be able to relate to the narratives of their parents.

As a result of these factors, remittance, which is usually one of the strong points in favor of skilled worker migration, usually ends or is significantly reduced with the first generation migrants. This is true since social ties decline with subsequent generations. It is a miracle if they go beyond the second generation.

MIGRATION THE UGLY

Anti-Migrant Sentiments

With the broken and rigged global economy, where one percent have ninety nine percent of global wealth somebody has to be blamed. So who do we blame? Some of the one percent are smart enough to pitch the masses against themselves emphasizing on the centrifugal forces that divide people rather than the centripetal forces.

Issues like race, religion, immigration are being trumpeted as causes of instability.

A closer and more intelligent look would reveal even within races and religions, reduced or lack of opportunities which is a consequence of disproportionate wealth distribution is the underlying problem. A number of factors have recently converged to fuel anti-immigrant sentiments and practices.

The global economic meltdown coupled with economic restructuring of western economies in the neo-liberal direction has given rise to moving away from industrialization and extraction of natural resources to knowledge, research and information technology.

This development has resulted in a slowdown in the creation of unskilled and semi-skilled positions. Many jobs are now outsourced overseas to countries in Asia and Eastern Europe with a lower cost of labor. Corporations believe that cost of labor is a major cause of increased production costs in North America and Western Europe. In their search for higher profits they have transferred many jobs in North America and Western Europe to other parts of the world.

This situation has resulted in greater competition for available positions among citizens and new skilled migrants with some people asserting that migrants steal their jobs.

Due to a glut in the supply of skilled workers and the ensuing stiff competition among them as well as between them and citizens, discriminatory employment practices and hiring vocabularies like "Canadian Experience" have emerged, especially in the larger provinces and urban centers. This policy among employers has put skilled migrants in seriously disadvantaged position and is a cause of economic hardship. There are some reports that more than half of poor migrants in Canada have entered the country as skilled workers.

Those without the experience are the new skilled migrants who are primarily from Asia, Europe and Africa. Some have gone to the extreme of calling it intellectual racism. The fact is that racism is not an open problem in Canada. The government and society officially encourage multiculturalism and inclusion. This is, therefore, an extreme reaction to a bad policy.

There are many stories of people changing their addresses or names to increase their chances of being called for a job interview. Having a certain kind of name and living in certain parts of the city is often the determinant of whether you would be selected for a job interview. If you are from certain immigrant areas, you have a small chance of being shortlisted, much less being called for interview or offered a job.

If your name sounds foreign or your address is where immigrants settle, you have almost no chance of being interviewed. I cannot count the number of resumes that I submitted in Toronto or the number of employment workshops I attended. I was never called for an interview except as a security guard, which I eventually did not take because I had to move to Alberta for my internship.

I had earlier trained as a security guard in Toronto. I loved the training.

When I arrived in Alberta, I did not waste my time applying for certain kinds of jobs even though I knew I was qualified and would do well in the positions. I ended up working as a night operator in the office of G4S, a global security company for about seven months while undergoing my internship training.

In what has been termed "Whitening of Resume", so many people resort to changing or abbreviating their names and using false residential addresses. This helps to increase the prospects for many people. I personally attended several employment workshops in Toronto where we were advised to change or abbreviate our names and addresses if we wanted to get hired. It is hard to imagine the psychological effect that involuntary identity and cultural change will have. Why is there so much talk about multiculturalism and inclusiveness? I will never do such a thing.

In the wake of global terrorism and unrest based on religion, race, culture and other differences, there have recently been incidences clearly demonstrating religious and racial intolerance. There have been people harassed for wearing the hijab. A woman wearing a hijab was beaten in Toronto while taking her kids to school.

I agree that these terrorist activities are condemnable and everything possible must be done to end it. I think it is a very dangerous attitude to generalize and to place the blame for the actions of a few on a whole religion or race.

The usual rhetoric in North America is that there is religious and racial tolerance and choice to do many things while developing countries permit religious, racial, and tribal intolerance. This is why America is called the land of the free. Therefore, one would have thought that North America would have grown beyond the attitude of lumping people together and painting them with one broad brush of ignorance on the basis of race, religion or some other factors. North America prides itself on a culture of individualization and dealing with everyone on their own merits. I think this is one of the most cherished values of American society, and one of the reasons that it is respected and successful.

People are smart enough to know that race is due more to society rather than to biology. In addition, for the most part, people are born into religion and do not choose their religion. Your family and religion of birth usually determine the religion which most people start practicing even before they can differentiate between their right and left. It is true that people's philosophy and perspectives are strongly influenced by religion and many lean towards extremism and intolerance in their religious practices. This is very disheartening. It can threaten relationships and social harmony and even cause disaffection and war. However, I don't know of any of the major, modern religions that expressly preach and support violence the way that these terrorists do.

It is true that people have the right to be afraid for their society, and they shouldn't let misguided terrorists overtake and destroy their culture and values. Everything positive must be done to stop this threat. However, grouping people together and trying to blame or punish innocent people for the transgression of others just because they belong to the same religion or race is not the solution. It may even expand and make the problem worse.

There is no longer a monolithic Christian or Muslim religion. These religions have hundreds of doctrines and sects. Their teachings and practices can be very fluid and heterogeneous. As a result, it is sometimes very difficult to group them as one or the other.

In the wake of global racial and religious tension, due to the terrorist attacks, race, religion and skin color are unfortunately assuming significant importance in the minds of skilled migrants when thinking of whether or where to migrate. This is a very negative development that is caused by terrorism. It is important to understand and know while it is legitimate and natural to keep watch and to take measures against these elements, we should not feed their expectations and desire to promote global disharmony. It is very surprising in this globalized and modern age, that some people think that you can just lock in Americans by building walls and keep people out to deal with your internal problems. Some people think that is the way to run America and still remain a world leader. It is very surprising that this position is gaining traction in the United States.

Canada like many other countries has enjoyed prosperity and expansion on many fronts to the extent to which it has welcomed migrants. If done right, we can still continue to make it a win-win game just as it has been.

No country grows by closing its doors on immigrants.

The world as a whole and the West, in particular, have made significant progress in this direction in the past five decades. We should not start to regress now.

It must be stressed Canada is not a racist country. As a matter of fact, Canada has deliberate policies to strengthen inclusion, diversity, and multiculturalism. There are laws in place against racism, xenophobia and religious intolerance. However, recent global events have brought about random attacks on Muslims and people of other faiths and religions. There have also been some "go-home" tirades on Muslims and other people of color.

Somebody asked me personally if I brought the Ebola virus from West Africa.

He asked, did you come with this thing?

I asked, "What?"

He replied "The Ebola virus".

"Yes" I replied.

He looked bewildered.

Then I continued; " what made you think you can disparage me because I am black?

He started to move away but I continued:

"I am sure I contribute way more than you to the society in any way you think of."

By this time, he had voted with his feet.

I pitied his ignorance, for many people sit in one corner of the world and do not get exposure and education about others. They have not seen other parts of the world. But at least they should realize those who could have the education, skills and courage to move to other parts of the world, fit in and excel should be respected.

Some people frequently advertise their ignorance. But while I may have the broad mind and exposure to understand this behavior in other people, not everybody does and this type of attitude creates a feeling of non-inclusion in minority groups.

The whole issue about racism is about people not respecting people of other races. It is all about respect. One positive way to gain respect from ignorant racists is for individual migrant to do everything to be well placed in the society. You should work hard to put yourself in a good position and leave ignorant racists to wallow in their ignorance.

It will be a tragedy if you have to be subservient to somebody who is racist towards you. I would not allow a racist or xenophobic to make my life horrible. Instead of capitulating to such people and systems, I'll reassess my journey and take an exit from that relationship the best way I can. It's a matter of pride.

Most skilled migrants are able to cope with isolated racist interaction from individuals because more often than not, this does not reflect the values of the majority of Canadians.

Where we will have major problems is where there is systematic racism encouraged by government policies. Fortunately, that is not the situation in Canada.

My candid advice to prospective immigrants is to cultivate open mindedness. Canadians are very warm and welcoming for the most part. Accept your new country as your home and mingle with the native born and other citizens as much as possible so you get integrated quickly. This will help you to achieve your aim of adding value to yourself and being a positive contributor to your new home.

It will not be too much of a stretch if we agree that there is racism everywhere in the world. If there is so much rhetoric about this in the United States of America, then you would suspect wherever two or more different races mix, there would be racism. This is not so different from tribalism where many tribes interrelate or ethnicism, when many ethnic groups converge. This is an issue everywhere in the world. The way this is managed is what matters. Mutual understanding and harmony among different groups can be cultivated and nurtured by deliberate policies and actions.

We know this, because in many regions and countries of the world, if the problem is not racism, then it will be tribalism, or ethnicism. This creates social problems. In Nigeria, there is tribalism, then when you go down to one state of the same tribe but different ethnic groups then you face ethnicism. We should, therefore, not pretend as if it is a color issue alone. It is a worldwide problem. It is my opinion that humans in a primitive state are wired to prefer those who are like them to others who are not like them.

The racial difference narrative is not going to go away. The discrimination between black, white, brown, colored and others is not going to go away. If it does, then humanity has lost its sense of color, its sense of difference and diversity. That would be abnormal. We should not pretend that those differences are not there, but we must recognize them and live successfully together with them.

Our duty as a society is to reduce to a minimum the proportion of primitive tendencies due to lack of education and exposure. We need to place less emphasis on superficial differences and more on the common features that make us one as humans. Our pre-occupation should be to enlighten ourselves, broaden our minds and be open. It is primitiveness, close mindedness, lack of exposure and education that promote a superiority complex, making people assess people in the context of color or race. It is primitiveness that makes a human prejudiced against another because of superficial differences like color or race.

Inherently we are all one which is not difficult for an enlightened mind to see.

As a white man, I should be able to say, "that black man" without any prejudiced meaning attributed to it and vice versa. That is when we become sincere. That is when we become genuine.

When I went through Wikipedia in December 2015, I came across a statement on allophilia, prejudice and tolerance. I could not resist noting it and will quote it here.

"The typical remedy for prejudice is to bring conflicting groups into a state of tolerance. However, tolerance is not the logical antithesis of prejudice, but rather is the midpoint between negative feelings and positive feelings towards others. Allophilia enhancement should serve as a compliment to prejudice reduction."[8]

This emphasizes the fact that when issues get serious bringing the stakeholders to come together to talk about it and continue to interact and learn more about one another is the way to go.

---

[8] Wikipedia, the free encyclopedia (accessed December 12,2015) https://en.wikipedia.org/wiki/Allophilia.

Therefore, our efforts should be geared towards public enlightenment, information and as much mutual multilateral exposure as possible so that people recognize these superficial differences, but also understand whether or not they matter. Those are not the main things that define us as humans.

What is most important is our individual values, inclinations and actions.

As simple as this may sound, it requires a concerted effort. It takes conscious efforts at self-education, social education and interaction to overcome this primitive human tendency. You need to educate yourself so you have a broad mind and be able to see everybody and every situation by its own merits. You must avoid generalization so that you don't fall into that trap.

It is the responsibility of society to teach the population that everyone should be evaluated as individuals. Generalization based on any criteria is primitive, unfair, and unjust.

Even if there is considerable racism everywhere, as long as there is no open government support, it is relatively easy to cope. Once there is no overt, systematic racism that is encouraged by government policies, the rest is easy.

It is most reassuring that most governments will not tolerate racist tendencies. This does not mean that all governments are taking active steps to punish or discourage racism.

It is evident that many citizens need to be educated about racial and religious tolerance. Have you forgotten about the vociferous, strong and ignorant voices of Americans who wanted President Obama ban travel from West Africa to America? Their protests were ignored and the White House followed a course of action that was a great victory for humanity.

It is almost impossible to feel physically and emotionally safe with the current racial and religious tension in the United States. It is important to understand, however, that these divisive tendencies are man-made and can be overcome or greatly diminished by our collective will.

Family Separation and Breakdown

A country is only as strong as its family units, especially the weakest family units. It is similar to the analogy of a chain being only as strong as its weakest link. It is, therefore, imperative that we make the family unit as strong as possible. This requires a conscious and concerted effort by all of us.

Many migrants move with the eventual intention of their spouses joining them. However, issues develop and family reunion sometimes take a long time. Sometime, it never happens.

This has led to breakdown of many relationships and marriages. Many have become involuntary single parents who continue to hope to join their spouses. There are serious negative consequences for relationships, marriages, families and the society at large. Many delinquencies leading to crime and jail are attributable to this problem.

Loss of Cultural Identity, Family, and Cultural Values

Migrants are expected to assimilate the culture and values of the new country while retaining certain features of their origin. Canada encourages this and prides itself in this diversity and multiculturalism.

However, not everyone is able to achieve the same level of assimilation with society. For example, the wife may adopt western culture and values earlier and more than the husband or the son or daughter may do so more than their parents. This lag in the speed and extent of assimilation sometimes creates division and tension in some families and within society.

Sometimes those adopting western culture too quickly and deeply are seen as abnormal and vice versa.

There are some migrants who might not approve of inter-racial marriages, changing religious affiliations or not even having any religion at all. These are usually not acceptable for children of first generation migrants. Tensions might develop when the migrant feels that his culture is being negatively influenced or diluted. This is from the migrant's perspective and has led to incidents like "honor killings" in some communities. Honor killings are essentially manslaughter.

Some migrants are charged with bigamy, which negatively affects them and their families. This happens because they do not successfully assimilate into the host country's culture.

In some cases, a male migrant man who is coming from a male dominant society cannot cope with a wife who is enjoying her new found freedom and equal status with men that was won through a hard and long fought women liberation struggle. The man feels that the woman is taking the liberation and freedom too far. As a result, tension erupts which leads to significant instability in relationships and families.

Some male migrants believe that there should be a limit to women's liberation. They view complete women's liberation as an illusion and believe that feminism is deceitful. They also believe that too much freedom may sometimes lead to instability. However, what is freedom and liberation when they are limited? There must be full freedom and liberation in order for it to be meaningful. Freedom is subjective though and varies in meaning and concept depending on cultural contexts and interpretations.

There have been many reports of male migrants killing their spouses. It has been attributable to the fact that the women had become "uncontrollable" because of their new found freedom and many of them were earning more than their spouses.

Some male migrants from other cultures find themselves in uncomfortable and depressing situations. They have come from a culture where the man is usually the breadwinner. They are also responsible for important family decisions. The unpredictable employment climate in the West can significantly change the situation. In certain cases, women can be trained for occupations that will allow them to earn more income than men. The man who is accustomed to his former status in his home country may be striving to improve his qualifications so he can get a better job. In many cases, he never reaches his goal. This affects the ego of both men and women and puts varying degrees of strain on marriages.

The right of women to earn a good income and to achieve equality with men is one of the flagship objectives of millennium development goals. It has been proven to enhance the quality of life and progress of the family unit and to improve the overall society. In addition, science, applied knowledge and education, freedom of religion, association, and choice in the way of life define western civilization.

This reminds me of a conversation that I had with my wife Eniola. One evening she had expressed concern about the many financial and business commitments that I had. She was wondering how I would be able to finance them. I tried to calm her fears by telling her that I would only pursue them if I was able to source the finances.

That made me reflect on the difference between when you are a practicing business professional and a wage earner.

Eniola: I can see you are still struggling to adapt your spending plans to that of a wage earner.

Alaba: What do you mean?

Eniola: Each time I see you want to handle so many financial commitments at once. I always feel you have been spoiled from Nigeria.

Alaba: Please explain.

Eniola: You were used to multiple sources of income and multiple spending outlets.

Alaba: Oh, I see what you mean.

Eniola: So you tend to forget that here in Canada, you have a fixed income. You still have the tendency to spend like you are in Nigeria.

Alaba: I am used to spending on many things at once but I never spend unnecessarily, however.

Eniola: Perhaps you need to review your strategy.

Alaba: I'd rather make an effort to look for more income. Instead of reducing my spending patterns. I am working on getting more sources of income so I can at least maintain this very modest pattern. This is very frugal.

Eniola: Hmm. I know it is a smart response.

Alaba: This is the irreducible minimum to make life worthwhile.

Eniola: I trust you. It's easy for you to put a hole in a line of discussion.

Alaba: You remind me of a story somebody told me recently.

Eniola: What story?

Alaba: It was about a Nigerian engineer who just divorced his wife; or his wife divorced him. Whatever.

Eniola: Divorce is not new. Perhaps they had their reasons.

Alaba: That's why I want to tell you the story. The reason, at least as I was told.

Eniola: I am all ears.

Alaba: Apparently, they had been married for at least 10 years.

Eniola: OK.

Alaba: They moved to Canada six years ago as skilled migrants.

Eniola: Yes.

Alaba: They have 3 young children together.

Eniola: Great.

Alaba: It took the engineer about 4 years to qualify as an engineer and get a position here.

Eniola: He's lucky.

Alaba: He earns about 9 thousand dollars per month and about 6,500 dollars after tax.

Eniola: Fair and typical.

Alaba: During the whole time that he was studying, writing exams and training to become an engineer, the wife had to take care of the kids at home, plus all the domestic chores.

Eniola: Naturally.

Alaba: Immediately after starting work, he bought a house, new car, changed his wardrobe furnished the house and all that.

Eniola: It is nothing unusual.

Alaba: And all this comes with great credit liabilities.

Eniola: How else would he be able to do all that with his income?

Alaba: Every month, he has to pay the mortgage and related expenses of 3 thousand dollars. The car lease, insurance, gas and related expenses take another 1,500 dollars.

Eniola: Yes.

Alaba: Groceries, snacks and related living expenses add another 1,000 dollars.

Eniola: Those are very expensive now.

Alaba: Then there are utilities, cable, internet and other expenses that total 500 dollars.

Eniola: That is typical.

Alaba: Suddenly, he realized how difficult it is to save one thousand dollars in a month.

Eniola: It is not a surprise.

Alaba: And the problem must be his wife.

Eniola: How? What do you mean?

Alaba: He suddenly realized if his wife had been working and contributing to the family finances, they would be well off financially.

Eniola: I am sure that the wife would want to work and be productive too.

Alaba: Question is, what work is more important than your wife taking care of the home and kids giving you the time and opportunity to develop yourself professionally all of these years?

Eniola: I wonder!

Alaba: So recently, the wife suggested that since her hubby is now integrated into his career, she would like to step out in the world and take steps to get into a career.

Eniola: Beautiful!

Alaba: At least with that kind of insinuation from the husband, that is the natural step to follow.

Eniola: Yes. After all, the woman is well educated and skilled too and will find her feet.

Alaba: But then, they have to pay for training, daycare and all that. So there is no way the husband's income would be able to take care of that.

Eniola: The good thing about this country is there is always student aid. They will help them with loans. The husband can also get loan for that purpose.

Alaba: You are right.

Eniola: But come to think of it, the wife has been shouldering the responsibility of carrying for the kids as well as him and the home. Even though she made sure that everything came out fine, she is getting all of the blame now.

Alaba: It baffling but common. It happens the other way too. Sometimes the roles are reversed.

Eniola: Yes. It is the cause of tension and disharmony in many relationships.

Alaba: The problem is with our mindset as skilled immigrant professionals. We hold this notion that once we qualify and get our entry jobs, we should quickly acquire all of these fancy houses, cars and furniture.

Eniola: Yes.

Alaba: We often do not realize that 6 or 7 thousand dollars a month is not a lot of money for a family of five in this part of the world.

Eniola: People should learn to take their time in acquiring all of these liabilities.

Alaba: This is especially true since many of these jobs are not even guaranteed.

Eniola: That's the scary part about it.

Alaba: The result is tension, usually two or three years later when the professional looks into his savings and sees that it is almost empty.

Eniola: That is, if he does not have a considerable credit card debt.

Alaba: Then he tries to figure out what the problem is. And aha! He did figure it out! It is because his wife is not working. So he suddenly becomes blind and forgets the contributions that his partner has made.

Eniola: Instead of settling down and calculating his income and expenditures so he realizes the problem is inadequate income, he puts the blame on his partner.

Alaba: Matters are made worse because there are expectations from folks back home. Comparisons with the material acquisition of friends, colleagues and relations they left behind, make them think that their situation is even worse.

Eniola: He must have forgotten that there was a four-year period that he had to be largely financially unproductive while he was trying to get credentials updated here.

Alaba: In addition, in Nigeria, they don't pay recurrent bills like they do here.

Eniola: Has he forgotten the trade-offs? Human capacity building, exposure, good infrastructure and standard of living, security and all that come at a cost!

Alaba: He has forgotten there has to be trade-offs. It is necessary to more or less begin again but it can propel you faster towards your goals depending on what they are, and how you make use of what you have to go about getting them.

Eniola: Back to the story. What happened then? I think somebody should advise him to take his time, discuss with his partner how to support her to pursue her dreams now. By the time she becomes gainfully employed and the kids get older, they will do well financially. Is that not what we decided to do?

Alaba: No. He did not take that long route. He is smarter than that.

Eniola: So what route did he take?

Alaba: He decided to start playing smart. He started flirting with a nurse. At least, nurses are fairly well paid. If he can get married to a nurse, then the days of his present partner upsetting his finances would be over.

Eniola: In Canada? Bigamy?

Alaba: No, divorce. He was going to divorce his wife. In fact, he has since realized they are not compatible, and that he should not have married her.

Eniola: After 10 years and 3 children?

Alaba: In fact, he was sure there was an evil following her.

Eniola: What about getting his partner into a nursing school? It will only take 3 years to get licensed.

Alaba: He would have none of that and, in fact, can't wait.

So he started gallivanting and flirting with a nurse. He was not discreet about it. There were Facebook postings of escapades and all that. After all, that will make the union hit the rocks quickly. Of course, the wife could not stand the open provocation.

Eniola: Why would she?

Alaba: Domestic violence and abuse followed. Hubby filed a divorce notice. Social services and women advocates got involved.

Eniola: You know those are not in short supply here.

Alaba: Employers also got involved.

Eniola: Aha!

Alaba: Her hubby lost his job.

Eniola: Ha!

Alaba: Case closed.

The moral of the story is that instead of having high expectations, skilled migrants have to learn to take things slowly, support their partners who usually would have supported them while getting their credential recognized, and do everything to stabilize the relationship and not engage in unreasonable comparisons and competition.

Narrowing of the Middle Class due to Capitalism

Canada has a commendable social welfare system, but what skilled migrant wants to be a beneficiary of social welfare? Skilled migrants don't want any of that. They want to be part of the workforce to contribute to the pool of resources to help the weak in times of need.

But losing their jobs is not an uncommon occurrence for skilled workers today. In fact, it is very easy to lose their jobs not due to the fault or misdeeds of the employee but because of company adjustments, restructuring and re-organization. In addition, the Canadian economy is not very large due to the small population, which reduces the potential for job mobility. It is not uncommon for people to survive on employment insurance or the government's monthly social welfare payments for months or years in order to survive.

If you are unlucky to lose your job in middle age, such as your fifties, you may be worse off. I have met several middle age people in job search centers. It can be very difficult to survive here. This is because the bills come in monthly and very few people have the savings to cover them for more than one year when they lose their jobs. There is no help from extended families like there is in third world cultures. It is very difficult to maintain mortgage payments and other bills with welfare stipends because that is not what it is intended to do. It is meant to help in lean times when there are few or no other sources of income.

You, therefore, see people have to give up their homes and downsize to apartments. Sometimes things get worse and they move to shelters.

This is not an economy where you can just wake up one day to start a new business because you just lost your job. You will most likely find yourself in a greater financial mess.

In my opinion, the North American economic system is rigged. All of the money is sent to the top, only a little bit is left for the middle class and little or nothing is left for the people at the bottom in the form of social welfare. Social welfare is good and is the lifeline for many weak people, but a society should do everything to limit the number of people on social welfare and that is called job creation.

As a result, there are many young men and women just coming out of the trades, colleges or university who are not even thinking of getting married or raising families with children.

Some people try to argue it is a culture, value and way of life and has nothing to do with economics. But I don't agree with that position. I believe most people would want to raise a family or at least get married in this very beautiful country with all its potentials. The many financial obligations including student loans, daycare costs, utility bills, insurance etc., are major dis-incentives to take on the added burden of raising a family.

It is my opinion that the Canadian middle class is disproportionately taxed which has to be corrected to breathe some life into the economy. Thankfully, the new government of Justin Trudeau has promised to address this issue.

It really surprises me that a country which claims to want to improve the welfare of women and children would not do more regarding the day-care costs for children. Canada is helping child welfare through its child care subsidy payment. I believe that more and direct payment for childcare cost is needed. It would be reasonable if Canada pays the full daycare cost for the first two children in a family.

This is even more relevant considering the demographic situation in Canada so the country does not want to have a population implosion. This is especially true because, due to recent security and other concerns, immigration as a means of increasing population may become a less attractive policy in the near future.

Individualistic Culture and Loneliness

The North American individualistic culture has its advantages. It can be argued that it is one of the reasons for the greater productivity in this part of the world. An individual's productivity is not usually hindered by some duties, obligations or societal expectations that are present in most developing countries.

These factors stifle personal growth and development in third world countries. However, most things have both pros and cons.

It is my belief humans have evolved to bond as against western culture that promotes individualism for its obvious advantages. The west however does have to cope with the fallouts and negatives of individualism.

An example is care for the elderly. In Canada, the care of the elderly, in terms of health care and other needs, accounts for a large portion of a provincial budgets. This is because healthcare is the responsibility of the provinces.

Loneliness is a common feeling in the West, especially when you get older. It is not pleasant to experience loneliness. It has huge implications on both physical and mental health. Loneliness is a public health problem in this part of the world. The situation is even more serious if you live alone; are unmarried or have lost your spouse. This is because humans have evolved to bind together and, therefore, loneliness is abnormal.

The individualistic culture has very negative psychological, social and financial costs to individuals and society. This huge cost can be drastically reduced by cultivating and nurturing extended family relationships and care system such as in Africa, Asia and even Europe etc. If you had experienced the communal living in those parts of the world, you would have seen how people in their old age almost always have younger people, extended family members or helps around them. There is the sense of duty and obligation of children or younger members of the family or community to take care of their parents and elderly ones. If you have seen that, you would not want to live the later part of your life in this kind of expensive and lonely life this society presents to the aged.

When discussing cultural assimilation, and benefitting from diversity and multiculturalism, it has to go both ways for mutual benefit and a positive experience. If the West would assimilate any culture from the developing world, I think that extended family culture would be the best.

Although Canadians are good, warm and polite people (which is very important), Canada and rest of the West should begin to explore extended family relationships. It will benefit everyone.

High Degree of Freedom, Personal Choice and Right Promoting Instability.

Freedom is good and there is nothing like it. Whatever we do, we want to be free to make our own decisions about how to go about it, when to modify our plan, when to implement our exit strategy and whether to quit or continue. This is true in relationships, business, personal lives, marriage, career and the pursuit of goals, or even with life itself.

Freedom is about gaining more control of your life. Therefore if you are taking any action or embarking on a particular course or project, ask how much more control over your life it will bring to you.

However, like everything that is good, there are also drawbacks to freedom. The degree of freedom has to be measured and controlled. In physics, we know if the degree of freedom of a matter is too great, it leads to instability.

Unfettered, unbridled or unguarded freedom is a recipe for instability and disaster.

Although freedom is good and should be encouraged, we must be mature, experienced, and open when exercising our freedom and rights. A society without a culture of compromise, give and take, and the knowledge that things cannot go right all the time will tend to have problems.

It would be great if people or systems would always meet expectations. However, we know that is not possible, even with machines.

Western society has a tendency to demand and expect perfection all the time. If a spouse makes a mistake, it can result in litigations, divorce etc. If the company manager takes a rare misstep, there will be calls for his removal. If a mayor of a city, owner of a business, the governor of a state or the president misfires once in a millions times, then it is time for him to go. The society leaves little room for alternative dispute resolution or only pays lip service to it.

This unrealistic expectation to always be right is resulting in an intolerant society that is difficult to live in.

Women liberation movements, children rights advocates, human rights societies, racial, sexual discrimination activists, animal rights advocates, green advocates and minority rights advocates have been very helpful in stabilizing the world and improving things for many people.

However, things are sometimes taken too far. Many marriages that would have eventually turned out to be successful, have not been given a chance because of organizations that would expressly provide avenues for divorce for a spouse.

People who would ordinarily have sat down to discuss things are not given the chance to settle their differences.

Good parents have lost their children to social services or foster care because of one or two transgressions trying to discipline their offspring. We need to tone this activism down a little bit. You get better results with commonsense activism.

Canada has approved physician-assisted deaths for some groups of people. This means that, in some situations, you can give consent to a physician to take your life. The Canadian Coalition for the Rights of the Child is advocating that capable minors should be legally allowed to give consent to a physician to kill him or her without the input of an adult. From all indications, that too may be approved in the future. Imagine what it would be like to have that level of freedom. This freedom in the medical choice would be very shocking to the average immigrant from the third world. This is not to mention the LGBTQ debates in the various school boards. What of the unruly gun ownership culture and the new paradigm of legalization of marijuana? All these things will baffle the new migrant from some parts of the world.

On my way to the library one day, someone hailed me. I later found out he was my neighbor. We had played soccer together the day before.

Neighbor: Hello, how are you doing sir?

Alaba: Hello, sir.

Neighbor: We met yesterday. Remember? We played soccer yesterday.

I am not very good at soccer but was at the school field close to our apartment the previous day and remember playing with him and his friends.

Alaba: Yes, I remember. How are you sir?

Neighbor: Fine. Where are you going?

Alaba: The North York Public Library.

Neighbor: That's good. Are you preparing for an exam?

Alaba: Yes.

Neighbor: Which exam?

Alaba: Pharmacy Licensing Exam.

Neighbor: That's great. I wish you the best.

Alaba: Thank you.

Neighbor: That is the right thing to do, man.

Alaba: You mean it?

Neighbor: Yes.

Alaba: It's tough for me because, the expectation is within a few months of getting here, I should be earning some dollars, but these exams are so demanding.

Neighbor: Young man that is the right thing to do. I've been here twenty-five years and I can tell you the best thing is to get licensed in your profession.

Alaba: Hmmm.

Neighbor: It is no longer possible to come here and easily get a factory, security, cab driving or other type of job. In the past, those types of jobs were fairly easy to find. That is no longer true.

Alaba: I can see this from my observations.

Neighbor: Yes, with the kind of education that most of us had from Nigeria, the best thing is to endure and get into an appropriate profession. Like I have said, I've been here twenty-five years. I was busy making money from those unskilled jobs. If I had another chance, I would do it differently, but it's too late to change now.

Alaba: Thank you very much for the encouragement.

Neighbor: I wish you the best. Wait for me downstairs. I'll drop you off at the library on my way.

Alaba: Okay, thanks.

He pulled up by my side and I hopped into the passenger side of his truck.

Neighbor: I am going to the hospital.

Alaba: What is happening there?

Neighbor: My daughter has just been delivered of a baby.

Alaba: Oh, congratulations!

Neighbor: Thanks you, but not a very sweet congrats anyway.

Alaba: How do you mean?

Neighbor: She is just in grade 9. She is 15 years old.

Alaba: That's quite young! How did it happen?

Neighbor: That is the question I expected you to ask. It's a long story, my friend. About one and a half years ago, I noticed she was going out with a boy. Of course, you know that would infuriate me. I scolded her and warned her to stop going out with him. That her focus should be her studies.

Alaba: Yes. That's right.

Neighbor: Just wait. I did not know she and her boyfriend had notified child rights advocates and social services.

Alaba: Do you mean it?

Neighbor: One day, I received a note from social services that they were coming to visit me. They came and advised me against scolding and talking tough to the child. They said that it would affect her mental health.

Alaba: I see. So what did they advise you to do?

Neighbor: You want to know?

Alaba: Yes.

Neighbor: You will be very surprised and may not believe it.

Alaba: Tell me: what did they do?

Neighbor: They told me I should give them sex education and enlightenment.

Alaba: That makes some sense.

Neighbor: I should buy condoms for them and teach them to use a condom if they have to have sex.

Alaba: Haa!

Neighbor: They actually brought packs of condom for me to give to them, in case I find it difficult to buy them.

Alaba: You don't mean it?

Neighbor: The result was that less than a year later; she was a pregnant teenager on my hands.

Alaba: That's not funny.

Neighbor: And nine months later, here am I a grandchild.

Alaba: That's not good enough. So you are the one to take care of them now.

Neighbor: Exactly. As a matter of fact, my wife, her mother has been with her in the hospital since yesterday, and I am going to bring them home now.

Alaba: That may not be good enough.

Neighbor: So I have to keep her with me. And when she's strong enough to return to school, she will. I just hope she would have learned her lessons and gets serious.

Alaba: I hope so.

Neighbor: How would you explain that with all these sacrifices? We usually say, we migrated here for the better future of our children. See what I am experiencing now?

Alaba: Yes. It's tough.

Neighbor: Let me tell you this. Bringing up a child is a major challenge in the western world. Most of the children do not turn out as well as we have hoped. In many instances, they do worse than their counterparts back home. How many children brought up here turn out to be professionals? Most of the professionals you see around are not born here. Most of them were even schooled abroad. They get here and qualify as doctors, lawyers, pharmacists, engineers and what have you. Most of those born and brought up here don't get serious and hardworking enough to get into these professions.

Alaba: You mean it?

Neighbor: Take that from me. I have seen children of immigrant professors who said they were not interested in going to school beyond grade 12.

Alaba: That's serious.

Neighbor: The value system here is very different from what we have back home.

By this time, we have gotten to the library, and have even been there for some minutes. So, I got down from the vehicle.

Alaba: Thank you very much for the interaction and the ride. Congrats once again.

Neighbor: Thank you. We'll hook up again.

Alaba: Bye.

Many breadwinners and husbands have lost their jobs for having a moment of misunderstanding and altercations with their wives, even when the wives and children have said that things are now okay.

Owners of businesses have lost them due to some video footage indicating some unapproved utterances and behavior.

Sure it's a good thing to have these societal checks and balances and freedom to invoke them, but too much use of this freedom has resulted in instabilities in our society.

We are now talking about terrorism and too many gun homicides in North America and especially in the United States. Why won't there be gun violence when people have freedom to buy unlimited amount of arms and ammunition?

Another example is the Internet. It has brought so much good to the world and taken us light years ahead of where we would have been without it. But while government should not be monitoring our private use of the Internet, there should be a limit to this freedom so they should know when it is being used for activities against our collective interest such as communicating and planning with terrorists.

We have to be ready to make compromises for our collective safety and societal stability.

The West, therefore, should look inwards and try to find a compromise out of this situation that is leading towards unbridled freedom.

People even go to extremes sometimes. For example, I have listened to programs or read about some activists asking for transparency on how the United States operates its drone programs! Come on! How can you have that and still demand a perfect security system? Yet, if a terrorist or violent gunman succeeds in one out of one million attempts to kill, we would be the first to blame the government.

The important point for skilled migrants is to understand all aspects of the concept and context of freedom so marriages, fatherhood, motherhood, family, jobs, business and other things can be preserved.

The right of women to earn a good income and equality is one of the flagships of the millennium development goals. This has been proven to enhance the quality of life and progress of the family with better outcomes for the children and society.

This coupled with science, good education, religious freedom, freedom of association and choice etc. are what define western civilization.

THE RIGHT THING TO DO — A PERSONAL REFLECTION

Migration has and will always be part of the global phenomenon. Skilled workers' migration, a modern arrangement is even better in getting the most benefit from this age long human undertaking if properly approached and implemented by all stakeholders.

The world stands to benefit more than it is now if certain steps are taken.

The following is what I think for the various stakeholders:

- The prospective migrant
- The source country and people
- The target/new country and people.

The Prospective Migrant

1. Do not migrate irregularly (without proper documentation)

Skilled workers do not usually migrate illegally, so it is not much of a problem with this category of migrants. Illegal migration by anybody is a recipe for disaster. Undocumented migrants undergo harrowing experiences in the hands of law enforcement agencies, employers, and even colleagues who more often than not exploit them in any way they can. Jobs are difficult to get. Even when they work "under the table", wages are much less than what they should be. They cannot access most government programs and services, sometimes even healthcare. It is an unpredictable, uncertain, and difficult life that is better imagined than experienced and you would not want to do that.

2. Be sure that you possess the skills needed in the target country.

What you often see advertised or stated on country's immigration websites or on the Internet, television or other media by immigration consultants (who are only in business to make money) is not the reality. To a number of immigration consultants, you are just a number. Their claims are not in tune with reality.

The reality on ground is that the data from immigration department or businesses that they work with to bring out their information are often not in agreement. Very often they lag behind the data from the different professional regulatory bodies and employers.

It is my opinion that they overestimate the needs of the employers and different professions. An argument that I have often heard is that if the skilled workers enter the country and are not able to find work in their specialties, they can find work in allied professions. What they mean is that if you are a doctor, even a consultant in your home country, you can be a healthcare aid worker. If you were a bank manager, you will be good as a grocery store clerk or as a cashier. An able bodied mechanical engineer will be good at driving the snow plow or grass mower. However, you need to undergo training for these "allied professions". Some of the training takes three to four years. This will derail you from the pursuit of your usual career if you would even think about returning to it again.

I have seen doctors who wanted to start all over to become a nurse, but were not allowed to do so once the nursing professional regulators knew they were doctors. In some provinces, there are many doctors who retrain as nurses.

Somebody in Toronto advised me to retrain as a pharmacy technician. I asked her why? She said so that I could get job quickly. How can a pharmacist retrain as a technician? However, this situation is very common.

This situation is the result of too much migration of skilled professionals. It is, therefore, very important for the skilled worker to look inwards, do his due diligence and investigate fully from trusted friends, and professional contacts in the target country before making the move.

I was advised in different foreign skilled migrant government organized seminars and workshops to retrain as a pharmacy assistant, or technician. What advice that was! Several reputable engineers had to retrain as technicians, university lecturers as elementary school teachers, if they were lucky etc. What a career setback that can be.

3. Do Not Resign Your Job or Sell Your Business and Properties Until You are Sure You Would Fit into Economic Activities in Your New Country.

Skilled migrants often resign their jobs, or sell their properties, businesses and even their homes as soon as they get their permanent resident visas. As we have seen, it takes time to settle in and to become productive in the new country. Some never get the jobs or the income to enable them able to regain these things.

This is a very common tragedy. What astounds me is how often it happens. People who are stuck in this situation often do not tell the truth to their family and friends back home or they never ask for the specifics. They suck it in and pretend that all is well. This dishonesty helps to perpetuate this ugly phenomenon.

Some have argued they prefer to be a taxi cab driver in the western world than be a mechanical engineer in Nigeria or a pharmacy assistant in Canada than a pharmacist in Nigeria. They argue it is better to serve in heaven than to reign in hell. They argue that the pull factors to the western world and the push factors from their source country, favors their remaining a servant in their perceived "heaven" rather than remaining a king in their perceived "hell". I agree that personal perception, philosophy, goals and aspirations matter. The "Heaven" or "Hell" definition of a place on earth is subjective. It varies with individual experience and values.

The reality is that many migrants come here and fare worse by any standards. This causes them to resort to self-consolation in order to preserve their psychological and mental health. If that works for them, it's okay.

4. Do Not Have Social Welfare of Host Country in Mind While Moving There.

While it is true that there is social and welfare help for residents of many western countries, skilled migrants are not usually a priority. It is important to remember that you must demonstrate that you have a certain amount of unencumbered funds in savings. This is part of the criteria they look at before granting you a visa. The purpose of this is to ensure that you are able to meet the financial needs of you and your dependents before settling down to participate in economic activities.

You, therefore, have to demonstrate that the funds are depleted and you need help before being eligible for public assistance.

Welfare payments and packages are only meant to take care of the most basic needs of financially needy members of society. These are people who due to one verifiable reason or the other are not able to meet their basic financial requirements. It is an excellent arrangement where the disadvantaged are protected and provided with a safety net. The various contributions of citizens, organizations and government to help ensure a just society.

I am sure that you do not want to leave your country where you are a major contributor to society who cannot only take care of yourself and

The Right Thing To Do — a Personal Reflection

your family's needs but also give back to society, only to relocate to another country and live at the mercy of handouts from the government. Most skilled migrants do not want to do this. The way to avoid that situation is to do your homework, and be sure that there is a job for you in the target country before resigning your job in your home country. This can be achieved.

5. Make an Effort to Avoid Family Separations

Many skilled migrants plan to come to the target country alone. They leave their family members and relationships behind with the intention of reuniting with them once they get established in the host country. The reality is that sometimes this can take a very long time to occur. In some instances, it never happens for one reason or another.

This has led to strain, mistrust, distrust and sometimes the entire breakdown of families and relationships with the associated negative consequences.

In my opinion, I don't think that the breakdown of family and relationships in search of better opportunities in another country is worth the trouble. I feel it is not moral, just or good for any of the parties that are involved. It leads to social instability and other types of social problems.

If you are married, try to move with your children and/or spouse or make sure that you do everything to make them join you as soon as possible.

6. Design an Exit Strategy

The beautiful thing about life is that there are usually choices. No matter how far one has travelled on a wrong road, it is never too late to turn back. This is a popular truism. Since I believe in trying out new things, I also believe that not everything you try will turn out as expected.

Success is a very good thing to have. Many people will identify with it. Failure, in my own opinion, also has its own upside. It is good to look at failure in a positive light because it usually serves as a turning point or watershed for future success.

This is why I believe while embarking on a plan or a journey, it is very important to have an exit strategy in case things go contrary to plans. The hard part would be when to begin to execute your exit plan. You shouldn't start too early because you don't want to blame yourself for not trying and waiting long enough for you to be successful. It shouldn't be too late so you don't blame yourself for waiting too long. With sound consultation and a sincere assessment of the situation, it is likely that you will realize when it no longer possible to reach your desired goal in the new environment.

At this time, it would be best to reassess your comparative chances in your home country and the country you have migrated to. If the odds favor your home country, the smartest thing to do is to execute your exit strategy. It is not unusual to adopt this reverse migration strategy. Many people have done this. They confronted the situation and have a very positive story to tell.

As a result, it is very important to develop an exit strategy. There is a saying "if going forward becomes impossible, then it must be possible to turn back." Putting yourself in a position where you are not able to go back when going forward or staying put is not working out is what you would never allow to happen to you.

I do not mean you should easily give up trying. However, there comes a time when it is crystal clear that certain things are not going to work out. Staying put in this situation is not the right thing to do.

It is necessary to be able to recognize these signs and to shift into reverse gear. No matter how far one has gone in the wrong direction, the smartest thing to do is to turn back. That is what a wise man or woman would do.

No experience is a total waste of time. There are many skilled migrants who have returned and put the skills, knowledge and ideas they acquired during their stay in the host country to use in their home country. In many instances, they have turned out to be successes. There are many examples of this type of result. When you travel, you gain knowledge, understanding, skill, expertise and have a greater appreciation of your culture, environment and home.

To Source Country and People

Skill worker migration can work in two ways for the source country. It can be advantageous or disadvantageous depending on how it is handled. Remittances have been recognized as a significant and veritable source of income that contributes to the development of the source country.

Sending skilled workers or any type of worker abroad is similar to an industry in major source countries including China, Philippines, India, Nigeria, etc.

The benefit is not limited to remittances. There are several other ways in which the migration of skilled workers benefits the source country. However, the problem is that many of the skilled migrants have left their home countries as a result of push factors which are usually negative. Some of these factors include: insecurity, poor job satisfaction, low standard of living compared to level of education, health care, social infrastructure, production infrastructure, etc.

Many of these source countries do not even have enough of these skilled workers to start with. As a result, skilled hands are moving from where they are most needed in the world to where they are less needed. It is a matter of them leaving where they are needed or where they are wanted. It is similar to the situation of the sick people taking care of the well.

The issue of brain drain has been well-documented. I think that source countries should reduce the effect of these negative push factors in order to stem the tide of this ironic brain drain. In this way, human resources trained with the source country's resources can voluntarily remain in their countries so they contribute to its development.

If this were to happen, some individuals would still migrate. That is okay, but the disproportionate flow would be largely corrected. This is nothing new but it is being repeated for the purpose of emphasis.

An example is the situation with the Nigerian economy. The problem has been a combination of corruption, bad leadership and bad followership.

Our society has not been successful in developing good leadership. Some progress is being made with the electoral process. However, the process has been very slow. There is still a problem with attracting the best, brightest and most patriotic in our society. There are still many problems with our electoral process such as quota systems, zoning, money politics, intimidation and godfatherism. This discourages the average patriotic Nigerian who really wants to serve from getting involved.

The sacrifice that must be made right now is too high for most people and the society is bearing the brunt. The question that any honest person will ask himself is; why would he have to make so many personal sacrifices like borrowing so much money, having a war chest of ammunition, political thugs and spiritual armaments and sell his conscience to his godfathers all because he wants to serve his country? He knows that once these factors come into play, he would not deliver as his conscience and talents would have let him.

An example is oil money and the other natural resources in Nigeria. Oil money is supposed to be the basis for an industrialized and diversified economy. It should have been used to secure a sound infrastructural and technological base for our society. This includes good roads, water, electricity, internet networks, telephone services, good healthcare services, a functional and practical education system, and all of the technologies and infrastructure that characterizes modern economies. These should be taken for granted in Nigeria by now, considering all of the petrodollars we have received. The full human capacity development of our citizens should not have been a problem.

Petro dollars should have been a fertile base upon which a very diversified and strong economy with sound creative minds and a bright future for our society was planted.

But what has been happening? This exhaustible natural resource, which takes millions of years to form, has been pillaged and wasted by our corrupt system. Our petroleum combined with our abundant human resources should have enabled us to successfully develop our economy. We know what happens to societies that depend on natural resources instead of tapping into the resourcefulness of their people. What is happening to us in Nigeria is typical. We can turn things around for good if we cultivate the courage, determination and political will.

Economics are driven by ideas and knowledge and not the extraction of natural resources and the buying and selling arrangement that we now have in Nigeria. Nigeria should be example of how a country can be developed quickly with the significant progress that was made in the first twenty years of independence. However, we are now the poster child for how a country can be under-developed despite abundant natural and human resources.

The world is now talking about climate change, reduction of carbon emissions and the search for alternate and renewable sources of energy for a sustainable environment. It is necessary for countries like Nigeria to respond to this now and start acting. If we are caught napping, we will be unprepared in the future.

The international value of a barrel of oil has been the dipstick for the global economy.

The price of oil has plummeted and may remain that way for some time. With this global clamor for alternative sources of energy, and the falling oil prices, it may not take a very long time before the value of oil as a global economic determinant disappears.

The world is moving away from extraction of natural resources gradually and leaders who think ahead are investing in the tertiary industry of knowledge, research and information technology.

Thoughtful leaders do not base the economic future of their country on the lazy man's economic policy of natural resource extraction. It is instructive for countries like Nigeria to look inward and to be proactive in looking for alternative sources of revenue other than natural resources.

Countries like Nigeria should become pro-active and innovative enough not to be left behind in this revolutionary wave for the sake of its economy and future.

According to President Obama "climate change is the greatest terror, public health issue, and challenge the world faces today". We need to get prepared for the future and put on our thinking caps as a people. In this way, we can create a promising future for our future generations. It has been said that "the best way to predict the future is to create it"

In our educational system, we need to move away from a tendency to produce bland graduates. They are not equipped to face the ever more challenging global competition. They are primarily just taught definitions and terminologies. We need to develop curious minds and critical thinkers. There are no ways to quantify that socially and economically. We need curious minds and critical thinkers for global relevance. The only answer to our question for growth, development, and global competitiveness might just be a question.

However, you look at it, the skilled worker migration program is a form of brain drain from the developing countries to western developed countries.

It is often argued that it is a two way traffic and back forth thing, which is not a zero sum game. Whether the source countries will benefit from the migration is very circumstantial and depends on the inclination, persuasion, conviction, and the prospect of the émigré in the new country. Therefore, it is not automatic. The possibility of sustained reciprocal benefits is very remote because the reciprocity usually ends with the first generation of immigrants. At first, the scale is gradually tilted in favor of the source country. This continues until the first generation is removed from the equation. From that point, the economic odds are in favor of the new country.

Nigeria produces skilled workers but there is not enough room to apply their skills. It may, therefore, be beneficial to continue to export this skilled labor and to wait for the repatriation of improved and added skills and wealth in the form of remittances, since they are very important components of our economy.

One very important aspect of skilled migration is that the success stories and positive achievements are highly publicized. This has a positive ripple effect on the up and coming generation since they try to acquire the skills of the positive examples. These serve as role models to them. And so there continues the generation of more skilled workers who even though do not eventually leave the shores of their home country, lead to significant increase in human capital.

Is it not ironical and paradoxical the western world that was preaching low fertility and birth rates 30 years ago are now coming to take away the products of high fertility from the developing world? There is the need to be original in our thinking if we want to get ahead of competition. Instead of paying attention to colonialism, corruption, capitalism etc. that perpetuate poverty, they were talking about birth rates.

We should begin to treat all our citizens as invaluable assets and resources that we will do anything to develop and protect. After all, they are our investments. If we give them up to another society, it must be for positive reasons.

African countries tend to be dependent and unsure of themselves. This has trickled down to the citizens which affects our psyche and keeps us from becoming independent.

Citizens should be imbued with self-efficacy so they can believe in themselves and the power to make positive changes in themselves and the society.

This must come from inspired leadership. Leaders should be able to inspire their citizens to break their limitations. Leaders should work together with citizens to achieve success.

Practical Commitment to the Social Welfare of Citizens

The primary responsibility of a government is to ensure the welfare, security and development of its citizens. It is a social contract, and some issues border on fundamental human rights.

However, many governments of developing countries, including Nigeria, have fallen short of expectations in their basic responsibilities. The nation's unemployment rate is at a record high. Nigeria is a very young country. It has millions of university, polytechnic, and college graduates who are either underemployed or unemployed. This is in addition to high school dropouts and trade school graduates who are not productively employed.

How would we not have low productivity in our nation in this kind of situation? Everything is dependent on the government. It is similar to the law of the jungle where the fittest survive and there is no help for the weak. The elderly and the young are in even worse situations. There is no help for the weak family. The strength of a chain lies in its weakest

The Right Thing To Do — a Personal Reflection

link. A society that has no safety net for its weakest in terms of their welfare and social needs is not a just society.

Many people go to bed hungry in Nigeria. There are no food banks. There may be some efforts to help the weak but these are usually too little and far apart. Many are homeless despite our culture of extended family relationships. There are also homeless and hungry in the West but what is the proportion? Most of the time, these are not people who are able or ready to work. However, in Nigeria there are many people who are ready to work but there is no opportunity to do so. Our, large, young population that should be a blessing we could harness for speedy development, has now become an albatross due to the lack of visionary leaders over the years.

In my view, taking people from being dependent and making them self-sufficient so they can fend for themselves as much as possible is the noblest of achievements. A society or government should create a conducive environment to support that as much as possible.

Practical support and the offering of assistance are more effective in improving the outlook for the youth and unemployed in our society than merely advising and sloganeering. That only offers hope and usually false hope.

Some people have a socialist orientation and can't stand to see people suffering so much amidst abundance. Some who dread the possibility of finding themselves in such a helpless situation have decided to leave the country. This they believe will save them from daily psychological assault of seeing fellow humans suffer while they hope to do more of whatever they have been doing to help.

No country should allow its citizens to travel to another country due to negative push factors for low job, safety or survival. It is the height of governmental and societal irresponsibility and failure.

Citizens should leave their countries to be better off in terms of their skills and economic status than they can ever be in their home country.

This should be what happens to skilled migrants. However, the reverse has been the case for most people in recent years, especially when you live in a country that is not in tune with global policy directions and aspirations. Many individuals, including professionals, are worse off.

We must do everything to reverse this situation of taking human resources from where they are needed to where they are wanted. A sick people cannot be taking care of people that are well.

Citizens in the diaspora and returning migrants have much to offer their home countries. They possess exposure, skill and knowledge, since many of them have undergone training and worked in the West. In addition to remittances, transfer of skills and knowledge, migrants possess the social and economic capital required to help develop the middle class and the service industry. We should, therefore, develop a system to harness their skills and contributions for the development of our home country. In this way, even if skilled workers migrate, benefits will continue to flow back to the home countries. This is how we can ensure that skilled worker migration is not a zero sum game for skilled migrant source countries like ours.

Followership and Dependents

For there to be good leadership, there has to be good followership. We need to be more visible and proactive in demanding accountability from our public office holders. Nobody places good leadership on the peoples' laps or on a platter of gold. It comes from a constant and persistent demand for it by the people. Citizens have to be constantly engaged with their leaders and be aware of their responsibilities as a form of checks and balances. This is the bottom line in democracy for the desired progress through policy and political re-engineering and quality improvement.

Persistence in our demand for good governance and accountability is the key. An informed public is one of the most powerful elements in a democracy. What matters most is informed public opinion. When public opinion is well formulated, politicians and public servants will have to adjust their attitude and policies to the public interest. The public, however, has to play its own role by making these demands. This, therefore, means that the public needs to be informed first. Ensuring that we have an informed public might be our most important responsibility. When this is lacking and steps and conscious efforts are not made to put them in place, people will deserve the kind of leadership that they get.

There are dependents, family and friends who are left behind by the skilled economic migrant. It is very important to appreciate that it takes time for a new migrant to settle in and become integrated into a new country socially, career wise, and economically. This is very natural. Therefore, migrants need the support and understanding of folks back home in order to achieve this. Integrating and settling in takes at least two or more years depending on the individual.

Therefore, unreasonable expectations, especially financially in the form of remittances either to help other people or even for the migrants' own purpose at home, is a huge problem and should be minimized. It is very distracting. This does not allow the skilled migrant to make the best decisions and effort during the integration and incubation period. Once the foundation is not made solid through patient and diligent preparation what might likely become of a building in future is elementary.

What Host Countries Should Do

I give kudos to countries that have the skilled migrant programs. Canada, in particular, is at the forefront of the points system for the skilled migrant program. For the record, Canada's skilled migrant program is considered to be the most successful of all the migrant programs globally. It brings in more skilled workers per capita than any other country and it is transparent. You can do your assessment yourself at home and know right there if you have the likelihood of migrating or not.

Generally, skilled migrant programs have been very beneficial to the world. Remittances, skill and technology acquisition and transfer by skilled migrants, global diversity, and multiculturalism are all obvious benefits. It also results in the creation of a wider global middle class, which is the fulcrum of a more stable global economy, fostering international understanding, collaboration and world peace. These are only a few of the positives that these programs have brought to the world.

The innovators of this idea deserve a Nobel award and Canada should be at forefront of who should win this covetable award.

However, the initiative can be made even more mutually beneficial for all stakeholders if we take a step backwards and honestly reassess the program for quality improvement and the delivery of the intended result.

For the most part, the program has been very successful based on different data. However, in order to not be guilty of the dishonest approach of cherry-picking data, we have to look at the whole situation. This will allow us to diagnose the problems with the program and to attempt to offer solutions. This approach will bring better dividends and results to all stakeholders in the future.

Success is easy to live with. It is at times dangerous, because you learn little or nothing from it. Continued success makes individuals or organizations complacent since we do not usually learn from successes but from mistakes. Therefore, it is very important to identify flaws in a program so that those who are responsible can step back and perform an honest assessment of how to fix any problems. In the absence of the proper mechanisms to do periodic quality checks for program flaws and to work out solutions, the bottom line, which is harnessing the benefits of this ingenious and innovative program for the mutual benefit of all stakeholders, suffers.

In this regard, the migrant target countries, including Canada, should do the following:

Ascertain the Need Before Bringing in Skilled Migrants

There are far too many skilled migrants who come to Canada without a great chance of ever finding a job in their area of experience, even if they qualify. The fact is that the intake of skilled migrants is far more than the country needs. As a result, this program which should be a positive experience for all stakeholders has become problematic. In order to assure transparency and trust, Immigration Canada should work closely with professional bodies and employers to generate reliable data that would form the basis for skilled worker intake.

The present practice of bringing in workers to slug out integration and to fit in among themselves, does not augur well for the image of the program and of the country. It is stagnating and frustrating for too many skilled migrants. This is breeding too much disaffection and dissatisfaction.

Most skilled migrants are very self-sufficient. They have a 'can-do' spirit. That is why they have the courage and entrepreneurship to even consider the idea of moving from their home country to another nation in the first place and also to be able to qualify according to the criteria set by the host countries themselves.

The procedure and processes leading to the "warehousing" of these talents is not well-regarded in the eyes of many skilled migrants. Therefore, it is very important for migrant destination countries like Canada to fully analyze the situation and offer solutions to the situation that skilled migrants encounter in their countries. The first step will be to be diligent enough to match their needs with the intakes.

Host Countries like Canada should intensify their effort to enhance quick integration of skilled workers to the economic fabric of the country by for example, making available training positions to prevent or reduce stagnation due to the lack of or insufficient positions as currently happens.

Paid internship positions. As a matter of deliberate government policy, government should pay for internship positions. This will help to quickly settle down the migrant for a productive professional and economic life for the good of society. Government can never go wrong with such an investment. The present situation where many skilled workers cannot secure paid internship positions is counter- productive, delays or retards their integration and does not portend well for all stakeholders.

Another measure would be to discourage discrimination in employment through the use of "lack of Canadian experience" as a discriminatory screening tool. While we understand that government cannot dictate whom employers should employ, the paid internship placements will take care of the lack of Canadian experience and therefore, this problem will be a thing of the past.

Canadians are warm, receptive and accommodating for the most part, but recently there has been an increase in the occurrence of anti-immigrant sentiments and activities. This indicates that some citizens still need more education and enlightenment so they are more accepting or receptive of new migrants. Integration and assimilation is a two way process.

People should know that assimilation has to flow both ways in order to be genuine and effective. The government has been doing this but should challenge people to learn more about the culture and values of other people. In this way, they can save themselves from conclusions and impressions based on limited exposure and knowledge thereby advertising their ignorance and bias.

Assimilation and acculturation needs to be flow both ways to be beneficial. By doing so, the skilled migrant program will further be a mutually rewarding experience and not continue to be a zero sum game for many migrants and source countries.

Canada should make deliberate policies to make skilled migrants spread out and settle in areas needing skilled hands instead of congregating in urban areas. This will require a balancing act and policies marketing this to migrants. Looking into this strategy will go a long way in adding value to the program for all stakeholders.

REDUCING GLOBAL INEQUITIES AND PROMOTING WORLD PEACE

The world's economy is rigged against poor people. I also feel that the world economy is rigged against poor countries.

In a system whereby individuals and corporations compete among one another to accumulate wealth and material resources, the weak have been left to their own devices.

Officially, the world's developed nations seem to be doing a lot to help poor countries to address the problem of poor leadership. They have been helping to promote the emergence of good leadership, healthcare, education, security, knowledge, industry, science, women and children's affairs etc. They deserve credit for that.

Some wealthy individuals like Bill and Melinda Gates, Warren Buffet, George Soros, Mo Ibrahim, Larry Page, Sergey Brin and Mark Zuckerberg as well as connected and influential leaders like Bill and Hillary Clinton have been trying to right the wrong of global inequalities.

However, much more needs to be done to help the disadvantaged.

On the individual and small group level, the rhetoric that has been coming out against the poor, disadvantaged and minorities has been disappointing.

We have heard of the Ebola scare mongering in the United States, for example. While nations and well-meaning individuals were doing their best to mitigate and stop the deadly plague decimating and paralyzing a part of the world, some who were supposed to be at the forefront of this noble undertaking chose to go the other way, and even went to the extent of campaigning for a travel ban from West Africa.

It required that President Obama, the White House and other well-meaning individuals to stand their ground against this inhuman campaign. Thankfully, the Ebola scourge is gone now and the good people have landed on the right side of history while shame goes to the fear mongers.

War broke out in Syria. Hundreds of thousands of people have been killed and several million have been displaced. This is, of course, due to the unfortunate poor leadership in that region. Women, children, men are facing a harrowing experience and are seeking safe havens from this inhumane phenomenon.

There were many people who were trying to discourage the nations and people of the world from helping. We have even seen American presidential candidates in one of the two major political parties making it their major political campaign issue.

We have heard candidates say that Syrian refuges should be kept out of America. Some have proposed religious tests to prospective refugees so they can keep only people of one faith in while keeping out those from another faith.

One has even gone to the extent of saying that people from one faith should be banned from traveling to America! As a result of this fear mongering, people have been attacked and assaulted. Religious centers have been torched!

There have been campaigns to build walls on the U.S.-Mexican border to keep some people out of the United States. One has proposed the opening of a registry for the adherents of a particular religion.

All these things are happening in the United States of all places!

This is the same country in which James Madison, John F. Kennedy in his book, many other American presidents and leaders, prominent and ordinary citizens alike have recognized the undeniable landmark contributions of immigrants in various aspects of America polity.

A whole lot of what America is today is because it has welcomed migrants. If America is respected and revered today in every corner of the world, one of the main reasons is its historically attraction to migrants as a land opportunities.

Canada too is following in America's footsteps nowadays, and as it is, in a more organized and measured way.

Thankfully, these fear mongers are in the minority. The good people who are in the majority in the United States of America will triumph again.

America has historically been seen as a welcoming country, and a land of opportunities where anybody who is ready to put in some effort would have something reasonable to show for it. However the rhetorics emanating from some quarters of recent belies this history. And personally, I am so acquainted with the history of slavery, the historical societal philosophy whereby the darker the colour of your skin, the less of a human you are, which still persists in some areas today, to be fully swayed by that history.

But we must at least acknowledge things have improved and can only get better if we all continue to work at it.

However, the fact is that, false rhetoric and lies, if left unchallenged, goes on after some time to be perceived as the truth. So all well-meaning individuals, and institutions should always rise to the occasion against these evil, primitive and ignorant tendencies of some. By so doing, good will always triumph against evil.

To be sure, fear is a legitimate emotion considering the wave of terrorism, killings, destruction, destabilization, displacement and other evil that humanity is facing due to the activities of a group in a certain region of the world. What's more, these people are doing all these things purportedly in the name of a religion. But I think that the world is wiser than to accept that ridiculous idea.

The world knows that those acts and ideas do not belong in any religion. Why some people who are supposed to know better choose to either ignorantly or knowingly play into the narrative and plans of this nest of killers just for political manipulation is what is so difficult to fathom.

The fear and hate mongering and where they are coming from have been very disturbing indeed.

Instead of spreading love, they decide to spread hate, instead of spreading harmony, they decide on disharmony and by so doing turn back the hands of the clock in global stability.

As a result, they increase inequality, poverty, disease, ignorance, and all the social ills plaguing humanity.

It is very important to remind these people that in the end, we will have nothing left to talk about other than our reputation and what we have said and done to humanity. We should, therefore, remember to do everything to protect it so we can end up on the right side of history.

It is highly unfortunate because due to this global trend of racial and religion tension, religion, racial, and other differential considerations have assumed a prominent position in the considerations of the skilled migrant when deciding if and where to migrate. This is a huge setback to a human endeavor that has been with us from ages and that has helped in promoting global diversity, tolerance, understanding, equality and peace.

A new man comes from within. Not from the outside. It, therefore, takes individual personal development, exposure, and deliberate effort, not to harbor racism and prejudice against people who are not like them—the so-called "outsiders". Our society can help individuals develop in the areas of education, interpersonal and intercultural exposure and interactions to reduce the ignorant tendencies of racists.

It is the sincere hope of all well-meaning individuals that these divisive tendencies against global peace and cooperation will not fester.

In all these matters, Canada stands tall in helping the victims of war and discrimination. We are very proud of that.

DOING IT RIGHT

Recently the government of Canada through the Canadian Immigration Commission made changes to the immigration processes and procedures for prospective migrants.[9] This is an attempt to correct the numerous obvious flaws in the program. It has been characterized by undue delays in the processing of prospective skilled migrants, and their warehousing, stagnation, unemployment and under employment when they eventually come in. As a result, this otherwise excellent program was becoming a scar on the image of Canada.

Therefore, the government reviewed the program and made landmark changes, which I believe was long overdue, but gratefully it was done.

The government recognized these problems and moved to correct them. As a result, all stakeholders can benefit from this undertaking. I think that this effort should be commended.

The recent modification is aimed at reducing processing times and expedites the economic integration of economic migrants through a:

- Federal skilled worker category
- Federal skilled trades category
- Canadian experience category

---

[9] Citizens and Immigration Canada; Immigrate to Canada; Immigrate as a Skilled Worker through Express Entry: (accessed March 3, 2015) www.cic.gc.ca/english

How It Works

After an online self-assessment, where prospective migrants' eligibility is assessed on criteria including:

- Relevance of skills
- Education level
- Language proficiency in English or French
- Job offer and prospects
- Age

They also evaluate other criteria. If you meet the minimum required points, you will be admitted into a pool of prospective skilled migrants, where depending on a job offer, and other pathways to become economically integrated in Canada, you will move to the next stage.

This underscores the fact it is what human capital you have got, what investments you have made in yourself and the extent to which you have prepared yourself that will work for you. The only one thing you can't take away from the program is its transparency and merit.

From the pool, you may be invited to apply for permanent residency if you happen to get a job offer or other economic activities. You will need to also meet the requirements of Canada's immigration law.

This new process is called the Express Entry Program for permanent residence in the economic migrant category. This is because the process is normally completed within six months.

The status of being qualified for invitation will be maintained for twelve months. After this, applicants have to re-apply to be re-assessed to enter the pool.

This is a fantastic amendment that naturally will prevent delays in the processing, warehousing, and stagnation of skilled migrants that is currently being experienced. This situation has prevented stakeholders from enjoying many of the benefits inherent in this program. Instead of bringing in skilled migrants and rendering them redundant, unemployed, or underemployed for years as currently happens, these skilled migrants would remain in their respective countries as potential migrants until they have an opening for economic integration in Canada. In this way, it will not be negative or threatening to personal, national or global productivity and integrity.

For a more detailed explanation, please visit www.cic.gc.

CONCLUSION

Bolu: So daddy, in all these, after all said and done. Looking back into these years you have spent in Canada, how would you compare yourself with how you were before moving here?

Alaba: Hmmm. That is a great question Bolu.

Bolu: And I am waiting for your answer.

Alaba: For one, I am a better professional. On a scale of 1-10 where 1 is the least level of professional practice and 10, the highest. If I was on 5 in Nigeria, now I am on 9 in Alberta, Canada.

Bolu: One.

Alaba: The travel, exposure, training, interactions, and the experience of even fitting into another country has instilled a lot of human capital into me. I can now practice at the cutting edge of my profession anywhere in the world. These things have had a positive impact on my decision-making skills and the evaluation of situations. It has given me a world view of everything, a broad mind, and a capacity to think globally even when I want to act locally. This is unquantifiable development.

Bolu: Two.

Alaba: And there are positive ripple effects on my family. For example, my wife has added a lot of human capital and development in many areas. I love it now when she discusses local and global issues as opposed to before we moved here. I guess, that is what they call exposure, and enlightenment.

Bolu: Three.

Alaba: And, of course, these would translate to the kids, of which you are one.

Bolu: Yes.

Alaba: But I must warn this is not typical of all cases. This all depends on how individuals see, process and apply the experience.

Bolu: But you agree that in your own case, you are a far better person in all ramifications.

Alaba: May be not all. I suspect I would have made more money, if I had remained in Nigeria.

Bolu: Let's concede that to you. It may not be true anyway, but I'll let that go. And by the way, who needs the money after all these?

Alaba: I agree with you. Who even knows what would have happened? We are only mortals. There are unseen forces that make it impossible for us to exactly predict the future. We can only work towards our plans. We don't really know.

Bolu: Exactly. You never know.

Alaba: I must add nostalgia is always there for me. I try hard to be at home here and I am to a great extent. Thank God for phones, and new and social media. The world is now a global village. So the psychological effect of physical and social separation occasioned by migration is generally much less today.

Bolu: That's right.

Alaba: I must say, I can't think of any other thing.

Okay, let me add his. The fact I am still alive today may not be unconnected with the fact I've been living here for the past several years. I really don't know. Only God knows everything and he deals with everybody as He wishes.

Bolu: And the fact you can put this kind of book together to help people make decisions?

Alaba: Yes! At least that's one sure thing made possible because I live here. I am also proud of myself and other skilled migrants. In fact, I see myself as the proverbial agama lizard that fell from the top of the high Iroko tree and was able to keep standing. It looked up the height, nods and congratulated himself even if nobody would. It was no mean feat. Yet this is just the beginning, by the special grace of God.

Bolu: Amen.

Alaba: In short, the Canada dream of the migrant or would be migrant can become beautiful reality.

Bolu: As long as the migrant is ready to do things right, getting things right is still a high possibility. Right?

Alaba: Yes. I say this because I trust Canada will always do everything to straighten things up and get them right. So if the source countries would get some things right, and the migrant do his or her due diligence, the experience can always be made to be worth the input, overall.

Bolu: Case closed.

INDEX

A

accomplishment 7
accumulation 30
acquiring 8, 81, 83, 85, 152
acquisition 8, 37, 45, 153, 182
activities 7, 43, 44, 114, 123, 139, 165, 170, 184, 189, 192
adjustments 17, 51, 121, 155
aesthetics 53
aggregate 5, 37, 42
alienation 32, 70
altruistic 24
anthropologists 7
antithetical 23
appeal 53
appropriate 7, 16, 39, 99, 161
asphyxiated 43
aspiration 5, 51
aspirations 18
assimilated 71
Assimilation 184
asylum 6, 71

B

behavior 45, 142, 165
Behavioral 14
beneficiary 39, 155
bias 184
borehole 43
boreholes 43
breakthroughs 39
busier 3

C

Canadian xv, 29, 30, 48, 70, 73, 75, 80, 98, 100, 101, 103, 105, 106, 108, 110, 117, 120, 138, 155, 156, 160, 184, 191
capacity 4, 17, 26, 37, 39, 40, 46, 60, 79, 90
capitalist 17, 22, 76
capitalistic 22, 130
circumstances 3, 4, 7
combination 43
commodity 3
conducive 38, 52, 123, 179
confess 3, 113
conflict 6
congregate 31, 32, 69, 70, 98
connotation 8
conscious 7, 37, 121, 145, 146, 181
consciousness xiii
consequences 1, 8, 19, 57, 81, 98, 146, 171
conservatively 48
considerations 15, 22, 95, 189
consultations 7, 51
contribution 40, 56
conversation xiii, xv, 48, 58, 77, 148
convoluted xiii, 26
corporations 19, 29, 122, 186
Corporations 137
correlation 38, 39
countries 8
creation 6
creative 45
crops 2
cultivate xi, 2, 28, 143, 175
cyclical 70

Index

D

democratic 38, 53, 61
demographic 5, 62, 157
department 168
dependents 55, 124, 170, 181
Dependents 180
destiny 80
developing 8, 26, 39, 40, 42, 44, 46, 56, 57, 62, 73, 85, 97, 122, 123, 139, 157, 158, 174, 177, 178
development 14, 38, 113, 121, 122, 126, 128, 137, 140, 148, 157, 166, 173, 174, 175, 176, 178, 179, 180, 190, 194
Development 100
digital interfaces xiii
dignity 5
diligence 75, 169, 196
diminishing xiii
disappointed 70, 77, 130
discriminated 70
discrimination 19, 32, 69, 72, 73, 143, 159, 184, 190
disillusioned 79
disproportionately 6, 156
distinguishes 5
domestic product 22
Domestic Product 24

E

economic xiii, 5, 7, 8, 13, 38
economic migrants 8, 15, 16, 17, 23, 58, 191
economies 21
economist 55
economists 14
education 8, 15, 17, 24, 32, 37, 38, 39, 45, 52, 53, 60, 70, 72, 81, 84, 85, 103, 104, 105, 145, 161, 163, 166, 173, 175, 176, 184, 186, 190
educational 38
emergency 133
encouragement ix, xii, 162
endeavor ix, xi, 1, 14, 15, 94, 123, 190
endeavors 7
enhancement 144
Enhancement 46
enlightened 8, 144
enlightenment 18, 32, 60, 145, 163, 184, 195

enormous 24, 58, 77
enthused 2
entrepreneurial 7, 122
entrepreneurs 13, 15, 55, 122, 123, 126, 183
enviable xii
environment 6, 37
environmental 53
equalizer 44
evaluated 13
evergreen xiii
evolution 6
expectation 16
expedient xii
expenditure 18
explode 3
exposure 18
expressed 3
expression 5

F

facilitated 44
family 7
financial freedom 85
free riders 39
freedom 85
fulfillment 7

G

generation 3
generations iii, 4, 6, 8, 40, 44, 54, 58, 77, 102, 128, 134, 176
Genetics 37
glimpse 6
gratitude x

H

healthcare 38, 41, 45, 46, 47, 48, 51, 52, 53, 132, 157, 168, 175, 186
heterogeneous xiii
hierarchy 6
homesick 70
homogenous 59
household 42
humanity 7
humans 7
hype 79
hypocritical 19

Index

I

ignorance 184
imaginative 45
imbalance 22
immigrants 4, 17, 24, 70
immigration 21, 25, 31, 32, 55, 70, 75, 102, 137, 157, 168, 183, 191, 192
impediments 53
inalienable 7
industrialization 46, 137
inequalities 6
inferior 8
information 168
infrastructure 8, 42, 45
inhabit 5
innovative 46, 56, 62, 64, 73, 176, 182
institutions 41
integrated 8
intellectual 44
intention 4
interactions 40, 194
international 18, 29
internship 88
inundated xii
investment 24
Iroko 196
Ironically 6
irresponsibility 8

J

judgment 7

K

knowledge 7

L

leadership vi, 60, 61, 62, 63, 85, 174, 178, 180, 181, 186, 187
legislators 63
legitimate 6

M

management 53
manipulated 19
material handler 95
measurable 7
mechanical 168, 169
mediocrity 26
merchandiser 95
migrants 8, 13, 25, 32, 191
Migrants Scout 23
migrate vi, xii, 1, 4, 5, 6, 15, 23, 39, 40, 64, 65, 102, 120, 121, 129, 140, 167, 174, 180, 190
migrating 13
Migration 4, 6, 18, 28
modifications 7

N

non-integration 69

O

opportunities 6, 8, 29
over-processing 3
overestimate 168
overpopulation 5
oversubscription 111

P

pasture 6
patient 3
pejorative 8
perpetuating xiii
persecution 4, 13
pharmacy 53, 169
philosophies 30
philosophy 170, 188
Physically vi, 65, 107, 134, 146
physiological 6
policies 3
politicians 43
precarious 9
prevailing 3
primarily 6
primitive 42
privilege xi
productivity 42
program 111
progression 74, 78, 79, 95, 124
propensity 6
proportions 6
prospect 95
prospective 4, 8

199

Prospective Migrant 167
prospective migrants xii, 29
protection 5
psycho-sociologists 7
psychological xii, 8, 14

Q

qualifications 8
qualitative 38

R

re-unification 4
redundant 193
refugee 5
regret 7
religious 22
relocating 1
remittances 18
resident 88
resourcefulness 28
retire 1
revelations 7
revenues 24
reversals 7

S

scarcest 3
screening 111
self-actualization 6
self-assessment 192
self-deception 20
self-esteem 6
self-sufficient 8
separates 6
significant 8
skilled migrant xi, xv
skillfully 18
skills 88
sloganeering 43
social 38
social alienation 70
social problems 15
spiritual 14
spirituality 1
stakeholders xii, xv, 31, 54, 73, 121, 144, 167, 182, 183, 184, 185, 191, 192
steal jobs 16

stereotyping 32
stimulate xii, 38
straighten 196
struggled 6
subjective 2
subsistence 2
supervisor 95

T

technological 39
technologies 45
tendency 5, 6, 7, 70, 159
tragedy 7, 133, 142, 169
trend 85

U

ultimate aim 7
unchangeable 3
underemployed 193
understanding 7
unemployed 43, 99, 178, 179, 193
unemployment 19, 178, 191
unenviable xi
United Nations 5, 80
unrealistic 16, 159
unreasonable 75, 80, 155, 181
urge 3, 48
urgency 9

V

voluntary 5, 7, 54, 90, 139, 146

W

wages 3, 17, 22, 73, 76, 167
Wages 21
western world 8
worse 9

Y

yam tuber 2
yams 2
yearning 3

www.ingramcontent.com/pod-product-compliance
Lightning Source LLC
Chambersburg PA
CBHW051051160426
43193CB00010B/1140